Rethinking Hindu Identity

Religion in Culture: Studies in Social Contest and Construction

Series Editor: Russell T. McCutcheon, University of Alabama

This series is based on the assumption that those practices we commonly call religious are social practices that are inextricably embedded in various contingent, cultural worlds. Authors in this series therefore do not see the practices of religion occupying a socially or politically autonomous zone, as is the case for those who use "and" as the connector between "religion" and "culture." Rather, the range of human performances that the category "religion" identifies can be demystified by translating them into fundamentally social terms; they should therefore be seen as ways of waging the ongoing contest between groups vying for influence and dominance in intra- and inter-cultural arenas. Although not limited to one historical period, cultural site, or methodological approach, each volume exemplifies the tactical contribution to be made to the human sciences by writers who refuse to study religion as irreducibly religious; instead, each author conceptualizes religion—as well as the history of scholarship on religion—as among the various *arts de faire*, or practices of everyday life, upon which human communities routinely draw when defining and reproducing themselves in opposition to others.

Published titles in the series:

Religion and the Domestication of Dissent:
Or, How to Live in a Less than Perfect Nation
Russell T. McCutcheon

The Symbolic Jesus: Historical Scholarship, Judaism
and the Construction of Contemporary Identity
William E. Arnal

Representing Religion
Essays in History, Theory and Crisis
Tim Murphy

Situating Islam
The Past and Future of an Academic Discipline
Aaron W. Hughes

Myth and the Christian Nation
A Social Theory of Religion
Burton L. Mack

Japanese Mythology: Hermeneutics on Scripture
Jun'I chi Isomae

Forthcoming:

It's Just Another Story: The Politics of Remembering the Earliest Christian
Willi Braun

Rethinking Hindu Identity

D. N. Jha

equinox

LONDON OAKVILLE

Published by

UK: Equinox Publishing Ltd., Unit 6, The Village, 101 Amies St., London SW11 2JW

US: DBBC, 28 Main Street, Oakville, CT 06779

www.equinoxpub.com

First published 2009

British Library Cataloguing-in-Publication Data

A catalogue record for this book is available from the British Library.

ISBN 978 1 84553 459 2 (hardback)
978 1 84553 460 8 (paperback)

Library of Congress Cataloging-in-Publication Data

Jha, D. N. (Dwijendra Narayan), 1940-
Rethinking Hindu identity / Dwijendra Narayan Jha.
p. cm. -- (Religion in culture: studies in social contest and construction)
Includes bibliographical references and index.
ISBN 978-1-84553-459-2 (hb) -- ISBN 978-1-84553-460-8 (pb) 1. Hinduism. I. Title. BL1202.J53 2009
294.5--dc22

2008032519

Typeset by CA Typesetting, Sheffield, UK
www.sheffieldtypesetting.com

Printed and bound in Great Britain by Athenaeum Press Ltd., Gateshead, Tyne & Wear

Contents

For Toshie

Abbreviations

AB	*Aitareya Brāhmaṇa*
ĀpDS	*Āpastamba Dharmasūtra*
ĀpGS	*Āpastamba Gṛhyasūtra*
ĀśGS	*Āśvalāyana Gṛhyasūtra*
AV	*Atharvaveda*
BaudhGS	*Baudhāyana Gṛhyasūtra*
Bṛ. Up.	*Bṛhadāraṇyaka Upaniṣad*
BS	Bengali Son (Era)
Ch. Up.	*Chāndogya Upaniṣad*
CII	*Corpus Inscriptionum Indicarum*
EI	*Epigraphia Indica*
Gītā	*Bhagvadgītā*
GobhGS	*Gobhila Gṛhyasūtra*
HirGS	*Hiranyakesi Gṛhyasūtra*
IA	*Indian Antiquary*
IHQ	*Indian Historical Quarterly*
KāṭhGS	*Kāṭhaka Gṛhyasūtra*
KauśGS	*Kauśitaka Gṛhyasūtra*
KauśS	*Kauśikasūtra*
KhādiraGS	*Khādira Gṛhyasūtra*
Manu	Manusmṛti
MS	*Maitrāyaṇī Saṃhitā*
PārGS	*Pāraskara Gṛhyasūtra*
ṚV	*Ṛgveda*
ŚāṅkhGS	*Śānkhyāyana Gṛhyasūtra*
ŚB	*Śatapatha Brāhmaṇa*
SBE	Sacred Books of the East
TA	*Taittirīya Āraṇyaka*
TB	*Taittirīya Brāhmaṇa*
TS	*Taittirīya Saṃhitā*
Up	Upaniṣad
VaikhGS	*Vikhānasa Gṛhyasūtra*
VasiṣṭhaDS	*Vasiṣṭha Dharmasūtra*

Preface

Hindu religious identity has been at the centre stage of contemporary Indian politics. Social scientists and political activists have engaged in a fierce debate over its different dimensions and have, in the process, generated a vast bulk of literature devoted to its ascendancy in the political arena. But they have not cared to examine whether the Hindu identity and the stereotypes that have been created around it have any evidential basis in early Indian history. The present collection of essays is a modest attempt to address this issue without claiming an exhaustive treatment of historical sources.

The essays that form this small book draw on my recent writings and lectures. The first two essays are expanded and substantially altered versions of the presidential address which I delivered at the 66th session of the Indian History Congress held at Visva-Bharati, Santiniketan, in January 2006. The third and the last essay is based largely on my book *Myth of the Holy Cow* (London: Verso, 2002), although it incorporates some new material as well. The three essays here have been brought together at the behest of Toshie Awaya to whom this book is dedicated.

While working on this book I have received valuable assistance from Malavika, Bhuwan, Shankar, Mihir and Vinit. I thank all of them. I place on record my sense of gratitude to Professor Niraj K. Jha (Princeton University) for making available to me material that was not available in Delhi and to Amarendra Jha for his input into the making of the cover design. I am deeply beholden to Professor Russell McCutcheon for asking me to write for the Religion and Culture Series of which he is the general editor, to Sarah Norman for editing the manuscript and to Janet Joyce and Valerie Hall for expeditiously seeing it through the press. I do not know how to thank my wife and companion Rajrani without whose support I would not have been able to pursue my academic activity.

D. N. Jha

Introduction

The roots of the notion of a Hindu religious identity is traceable to the nineteenth century when the colonial state and its administrative apparatus codified and reified the religious and caste divisions prevalent in India. The beginning of the census operations in 1872, the application of categories of "Hindus" and "Muhammadans" to classify and divide the people of the Indian colony on religious lines and to keep these religious groups constantly at loggerheads arguably played a crucial role in creating the notion of a Hindu identity as distinct from Muslim or Christian. But an equally, if not more, important factor in the initial phase of its construction was the acceptance and dissemination of the term "Hindu" by religious thinkers and reformists of the nineteenth century. Ram Mohan Roy (1772–1833), who founded the Brahmo Samaj in 1828, vindicated Hinduism against the expansion of Christianity, even though he was in favour of certain Western reformist ideas such as the abolition of *sati*. The religion based on the Vedas and Upaniṣads, he argued, was monotheistic and egalitarian, and it was only over the course of time that decline set in and retrograde practices such as polytheism, the caste system and the suppression of women crept into it. The notion of the Vedic age as a "golden age" was thus "embodied in the doctrine of the Brahmo Samaj" (Jaffrelot 2007: 7–8) and it anticipated the ideas of subsequent religious reformers. Dayananda Saraswati (1824–1883), who founded the reformist organization Arya Samaj in 1875, also harked back to the Vedic golden age in Āryāvarta where the first men were born and where Sanskrit, the mother of all tongues, was spoken (Jordens 1978: 110), and "maintained that the 'Aryas' of the Vedas were the autochthonous people of Bhārat" (Jaffrelot 2007: 9). Unlike Roy, he treated the Vedas as a divine revelation and accorded them the status of a fixed and clearly demarcated canon—a status which the Bible and Quran enjoyed in Christianity and Islam respectively. This gave a "specifity and distinction" to the Arya Samajist ideology in relation to Hinduism which, according to it, was a degraded form of Vedic religion—a reason why the followers of Dayananda preferred to register themselves as "Aryas" and not Hindus in the 1891 Punjab census (Jones 1981: 87). Apparently thus Dayananda would not initially appear to be a proponent of Hindu nationalism but, judging from his activities, he was certainly a forerunner of later Hindu chauvinism and xenophobia. For example, his concern for cow-protection, which became an important item on the militant Hinduism's agenda in the course of time, was evident early in his career. It became pronounced from 1877 when he began to devote special lectures to it and culminated in his founding the Gorakhsini Sabha in 1881. So deep was his involvement in the movement for cow-protection that despite the sharp ideological antagonism with the adherents of the anti-reformist and orthodox Brāhamaṇical religious practices called the Sanatanists, the Arya Samajists felt no uneasiness of conscience in collaborating with them over the issue. This projected the protection of the cow as a collective responsibility of a wide cross-section of the people and galvanized and unified them as Hindus (Zavos 2000: 87–88) and strengthened their separate identity as against that of the Muslims who were stereotyped as kine killers and beef eaters. Similarly, Dayananda's concern for the purification/reconversion (*śuddhi*) of those who or whose ancestors had converted to Islam and Christianity and their reacceptance into the Aryan/Hindu fold (Llewellyn 1993: 99–103; Zavos 2000: 87–92), clearly recognized the followers of these religions as enemies. Though initially opposed by the orthodox Sanatanists who projected Hinduism as a non-proselytizing religion[1] it received endorsement from them (e.g. Madan Mohan Malaviya) in the early twentieth century and thus tended to reinforce the idea of Hindu identity.

Some of the ideas of Dayananda found an echo in those of Vivekananda (1863–1902), though his background and career trajectory were different from those of his predecessors. Like them, he glorified the Vedas and Upaniṣads, and referred nostalgically to the earliest period of Indian past as one of "Vedic harmony"—a period when the people were "ruled according to the principles of the Vedas and India enjoyed 2000 years of uninterrupted peace, tranquility and prosperity" (Misra 2004: 37); in contrast, he spoke, with a *cri de coeur*, of the period of the Muslim rule as one of the oppression of the Hindus. Although he did not share the concern of Dayananda for cow-protection, like him, he was interested in converting members of other faiths to his own which in his case was the Advaita Vedānta and which he used to unify the Hindus. He founded the Rama Krishna Mission in 1897 for its promotion and propagation through Maths and Ashrams in different parts of India as well as through international missionary activity (Brekke 2002: 47). Despite their different views on issues relating to social and religious reform, Dayananda and Vivekananda shared a revivalist perception of India's past and an exclusivist notion of Hinduism, which were echoed by their contemporaries in different parts of the country. In Bengal, Rajnarain Basu (1826–1899), a close associate of Debendranath Tagore, stood for the triumph of *Sanātana dharma*, spoke forcefully of the superiority of Hindu religion and culture in contrast to Christainity and Islam and asserted that "his Hindu Mahasamiti...could not have a place for Muslims" (Bhatt 2001: 24). Similarly, Chandranath Basu (1844–1910), who was intimate to Bankim Chandra Chattopadhyaya and was a champion of reform through revivalism, published his *Hindutva—An Authentic History of Hindus* in Bengali as early as 1892 in which he portrayed Hinduism "in terms of its glorious archaic past" and as superior to Christianity, and presented his spirited defence of traditional Brāhmaṇical ritualism, child marriage, caste system, patriarchal values, and so on (Bhatt 2001: 25–6). Essentially anti-Islamist at the core, the Hindutva[2] idea popularized by him was conspicuously present in Bankim Chandra's (1838–94) influential novel *Ānandamaṭh* (1882), which refers to Muslims as "dirty bastards" (Sarkar 1996: 175).[3]

The demonization of Muslims was a prominent theme also in the works of many late nineteenth-century writers. In Hindi, Bharatendu Harishchandra (1850–85) depicted Muslim characters as cruel, cowardly, treacherous, bigots and depraved, and his contemporaries described Muslim rule "as a chronicle of rape and abduction of Hindu women, the slaughter of sacred cows, and the defilement of temples" (Hasan 1996: 200). The Marathi writers displayed a similar attitude to Muslims and described them as "bullies and fanatics" and the period of their rule as one of "the overall degradation of the Hindus" and of the spread of the "pernicious influence of Islam on their social customs" (Hasan 1996: 200). The most influential of the Marathi writers was the nationalist and social reformer Bal Gangadhar Tilak (1856–1920), who made "a conscious choice of historical figures and symbols" to strengthen the notion of a Hindu identity (Hasan 1996: 200). He reinvented a largely domestic festival of Ganesh by giving it a group character and used it as an instrument for mobilizing the Hindus. He revived the memories of Shivaji, promoted the celebration of Shivaji festivals and projected him as a pre-eminent symbol of Hindu militancy against Muslims. In 1893 he founded the Anti-Cow Killing Society and gave a direct challenge to Muslims. While Tilak thus sought to build an aggressive Maratha/Hindu identity leading often to Hindu–Muslim antagonism and tension, he emphatically asserted that the essence of Hinduism lay in its metaphysics and tolerance of other faiths (Sathe 1994: 166), though judging by his anti-Muslim sentiments and activities, these were mere fine words. His writings on the history of ancient Indian culture,[4] therefore, dwelt on Hindu–Aryan primordialism and supported his notion of a future Hindu nation. He pushed the date of the Vedic period from 1500 BCE first to 4000 BCE and then to 8000 BCE, glorified the Vedic Aryan race and religion and wove "a thread of cultural and religious continuity between the Aryans of the furthest antiquity and present-day Hindus" (Kaiwar 2003: 45). Despite his view that the original home of the Aryans was in the Arctic, he underlined the importance of the

Vedic Aryan heritage. "During Vedic times," Tilak asserted, "India was a self-contained country...united as a great nation...". He loudly proclaimed that the "common factor" in Indian society was "the feeling of Hindutva" and that all "hindus were one because of their adherence to *Hindudharma*" (Bhatt 2001: 36; Kaiwar 2003: 45). Based on his reading of the *Bhagvadgītā* on which he wrote an elaborate commentary, he espoused the use of violence as a higher duty (Minor 1991: 44–60). Tilak's ideas, especially his anti-Muslim sentiments, assertion of Aryan/Hindu primordial identity, and his apologia for the use of violence had many takers during the extremist phase of India's freedom struggle, the most important of them being Aurobindo who declared that the Hindu religion was the eternal religion (*sanātana dharma*) preserved by the Aryan race through centuries, equated it with nationalism, and, inspired by the *Gītā* like Tilak, justified the use of violence in its defence and in the nationalist resistance to the British rule (Kaiwar 2003: 42; Minor 1991: 61–87). It was, however, Tilak who was really the forerunner of militant Hinduism of subsequent years expounded by V. D. Savarkar (1883–1966), K. B. Hedgewar (1889–1940) and M. S. Golwalkar (1906–1973) and others in the wake of an unprecedented communalization of Indian politics from the 1920s onwards.

V. D. Savarkar, seven-times president of the Hindu Mahasabha, the right-wing Hindu political party, and founder of the modern-day Hindutva movement, sought to provide a comprehensive definition of Hindu identity in his *Hindutva/Who is a Hindu?* published in 1923 and in doing so he borrowed and elaborated several ideas of Tilak's with whom he came in contact early in life. Although Tilak's commitment to the anti-cow slaughter movement was not much of an attraction for Savarkar, the Hindutva idea, to which Tilak had referred, became the central theme of his work in which he postulated that it was Hindutva (= Hinduness), rather than Hinduism, that constituted Hindu identity. But Hindutva itself, he tells us, "defies all attempts at analysis... [it] is not a word but a history. Not only the spiritual or religious history of our people, but a history in full" (Savarkar 2005 [1923]: 3). Like Tilak, he accepted the belief that the Aryans originated outside India, migrated into the modern Punjab and called themselves Hindu (or Sindhu) for the first time and spread out to different parts of the subcontinent, giving birth to a common race of the Hindus through miscegenation of Aryans and non-Aryans, and creating new "colonies" on the way until the day Rāma made his triumphant entry into Ceylon, the day which was "the real birth-day of our Hindu people" (Savarkar 2005 [1923]: 11–12; Bhatt 2001: 87). On the one hand Savarkar primordialized Hindu identity and asserted that "the word Hindu dates its antiquity from a period...that even mythology fails to penetrate—to trace it to its source" (Savarkar

2005 [1923]: 10); and, on the other, he declared that it was during the mediaeval period that Hindus "were welded into a nation to an extent unknown in our history" as a result of their "struggle of life and death" against the "Muslim invaders" and "tyrants." Despite his deeply flawed perception of history, however, he insisted that Hindus are a nation and India must be a land reserved for them. A Hindu, according to Savarkar, was one (i) who acquired citizenship by paternal descent, i.e., who was born in India, (ii) who was born of Hindu parents and thus possessed Vedic Aryan blood and (iii) who shared a common *sanskriti* (culture) "suggestive...of that language, Sanskrit, which has been the chosen means of expression and preservation of that culture, of all that was best and worth-preserving in the history of our race" (Savarkar 2005 [1923]: 92). In the ultimate analysis, however, a Hindu, according to Savarkar, was one who regarded India as his fatherland (*pitribhūmi*) and holy land (*puṇyabhūmi*) (Savarkar 2005 [1923]: 115), one whose religion must have grown "out of the soil of India." This definition of a Hindu excluded Muslims and Christians whose holy lands were in Arabia and Palestine respectively and who were inherently treacherous. Savarkar's Hindu supremacism, not surprisingly, was best summed up in his call to "Hinduise all politics and Militarise all Hindudom"—a call that was to become a rallying cry of Hindu identity and nationalism.

Two years after Savarkar expounded his concept of Hindutva, Keshav Baliram Hedgewar (1889–1940), a Maharashtrian brāhmaṇ of Tilakite association, drawing inspiration from him but going a step further than him, proclaimed that long before the recorded history, the Hindus were a mighty and prosperous nation and they ruled "over vast regions of the earth and our flag flew over many lands" (Kanungo 2002: 42). But his real importance in promoting militant Hindu identity lay not in his ideas articulated through his occasional writings and speeches but in the fact that in 1925 he founded the Rashtriya Svayamsevak Sangh (National Volunteer Corps), popularly known as the RSS, whose network has grown steadily over the years (Jaffrelot 1996; 2005) and has now a large number of bodies including political parties affiliated to it. This organization, since its inception, has stood for a martial brand of Hinduism buttressed by its hierarchical and dictatorial organizational structure, and the daily morning/evening meeting of its basic unit called *shākhās* (branch) where the young recruits are imparted physical and mental training more or less on the model of the traditional *akhārā*, a place where "the young men of a locality gather daily for body building, exercise and sports—mainly wrestling and weight-lifting" (Jaffrelot 2005: 2–5, 56–102). It has indeed remained the vanguard of the Hindutva movement until our own times and has had its hand, directly or through its affiliates, in several communal conflagrations.

While Savarkar provided an ideological *raison d'être* of the RSS, Hedgewar, supposedly endowed with supreme organizational skills, gave it a para-military and fascist character. It was, however, for M. S. Golwalkar, who succeeded him in 1940 as chief of the RSS, to give it "the ideological charter it had previously lacked" (Jaffrelot 2005: 97). In 1939, a year before he took over from Hedgewar as the second chief of the RSS, he published his *We Or Our Nationhood Defined*[5] and the collection of his essays and speeches was published in 1966 as *Bunch of Thoughts*. While Savarkar had claimed that the Hindu race originated four thousand years ago, in his writings Golwalkar, much like Tilak, pushed back its antiquity by 80–100 centuries. Inspired by Hitler's ethnic nationalism he rejected the view that the Hindu–Aryans have been exogenous to India and asserted that "we Hindus came into this land from nowhere, but are indigenous children of the soil always, from time immemorial and are natural masters of the country" (Golwalkar 1939: 6). It was from this indigenist Hindu–Aryan position that he asserted that "the foreign races in Hindusthan must either adopt the Hindu culture and language, must learn to respect and hold in reverence Hindu religion, must entertain no ideas but those of glorification of the Hindu race and culture...or may stay in the country, wholly subordinated to the Hindu nation, claiming nothing, deserving no privileges, far less any preferential treatment—not even citizen's rights" (Golwalkar 1939: 62). Deeply committed to the supremacy of the Hindu religion and culture, Golwalkar enunciated his notion of "cultural nationalism" which was distinct from Savarkar's "territorial nationalism" and which, in his scheme of things, made it obligatory for Muslims and other religious minorities to respect and revere the Hindu religion. Unlike Savarkar, he attached great importance to the protection of the cow and considered this animal as "mother" and the emblem of Hindu devotion and protested against its slaughter (Golwalkar 1966: 59, 232, 363). According to him, the Muslims began the practice of cow killing in India and the British continued it and since the practice began with foreign domination "it is a stigma on us" (Golwalkar 1966: 496). Despite some differences in their ideas and attitude, both Savarkar and Golwalkar emphasized, in varying degrees, the primordialization and indigenization of Hindu identity. They also demonized religious minorities, especially the Muslims—a tendency whose pugnacious manifestations in the post-Neruvian India culminated in the demolition of the sixteenth-century Muslim mosque at Ayodhya in 1992 triggering countrywide Hindu–Muslim riots and the genocide of Muslims in Gujarat in 2002 putting the country to shame. Even so the RSS and its affiliates (whose number has swelled over the years) always deny their objective of establishing a religious

Hindu state and claim "Hinduism as a universalistic and tolerant religious philosophy" (Kanungo 2002: 126).

The divisive concept of Hindu identity propagated by social and religious reformers, nationalist leaders and cultural nationalists has received much institutional support from the modern Indian university system and has found a prominent place in academic histories since the early twentieth century—a fact which calls for a detailed study but a few quick examples should serve our purpose here. Thus the Calcutta University, the first modern university in India, established separate departments of ancient Indian history and culture and Islamic history, the first giving a boost to the supposed glories of ancient India and the second to the denigration of Muslims. Many universities established after the one in Calcutta followed suit and set up separate departments for teaching and research in ancient Indian history and culture. This discouraged the study of an integrated history of the country, and encouraged the growth of a retrograde and revivalist historiography with primordialization and glorification of the Aryan/Hindu identity as its main agenda. Thus almost at the same time as Savarkar was busy defining the contours of Hindu identity, Abinash Chandra Das, lecturer in ancient Indian history and culture in Calcutta University, argued that the Aryans were the original inhabitants of Sapta-Sindhu (modern Punjab) which, according to him, was "the oldest life-producing region in the whole of the Indian subcontinent," and assigned the Ṛgvedic hymns to 25,000 years ago or the Pleistocene (Das 1971 [1920]: 22–23).

A majority of historians writing during the period of nationalist resistance to the British rule as well as after India's independence betray a strong bias in favour of the Aryan autochthony and the fantastic antiquity of the Aryan heritage. Even those historians who seem to have remained uninfluenced by these ideas have not freed themselves from a nostalgia for the ancient—or, what has traditionally been called the Hindu—period. Important among them are K. P. Jayaswal, H. C. Raichaudhari, K. A. Nilakanta Sastri, and R. C. Majumdar, who has been the most influential and prolific among them and whose writings are replete with Hindu revivalist and anti-Islamist ideas. A persistently polemic apologist of the greatness of ancient "Hindus" and a firm believer in the hinduization of the south-east Asian countries, Majumdar ignored their indigenous cultures and thus lent an ideological support to Hedgewar's vacuous claim that the Hindu "flag flew over many lands." As general editor of the multi-volume publication *History and Culture of the Indian People*, he devoted more volumes to what he considered to be the periods of Hindu domination and fewer volumes to those that he considered to be periods of Muslim domination (Sharma 1990: 6). He credited the Hindus for their "spirit of religious toleration" and denigrated the Muslims for their intolerant and oppressive rule and for destroying Hindu temples. A similar, but stronger, anti-Muslim attitude is seen in the works of Jadunath Sarkar who wrote extensively on mediaeval Indian history. Like Majumdar, he perceived the mediaeval period of Indian history as one of perpetual confrontation between the Hindus and Muslims and, according to him, the ideal of the Mughal state was "the conversion of the entire population to Islam." Listing all the individual acts of omission and commission during the five hundred years of "Muslim rule," he presented a negative picture of Muslim rulers (Srivastava 1989: 86) and spoke in glowing terms of the resistance to Muslims by Shivaji who, as a symbol of Maratha/Hindu chauvinism, has been a significant factor in even contemporary Indian politics—so much so that any critical reference to him may prove perilous! "Shivaji," Jadunath Sarkar tells us, "has shown that the tree of Hinduism is not really dead, that it can rise from beneath the seemingly crushing load of centuries of political bondage" (Sarkar 1973: 390). The attitude of Majumdar and Sarkar and other scholars of their ilk has led to the perception of Muslims as oppressors and inherently intolerant and opposed to Hindus who, as a contrast, are looked upon as weak and tolerant. An interesting example of this stereotyping is the depiction of Hindus as vegetarians and of Muslims as beef-eaters. A historian of mediaeval India, for example, tells us that "the Hindus in general were vegetarians... and abhorred beef" and "the Muhammadans, on the other hand, were almost cent [*sic*] per cent non-vegetarians, and were not prepared to give up cow-slaughter and beef-eating" (Srivastava 1984: vii). While the clichés about the Muslims created by right-wing politicians and scholars calls for a separate rigorous scrutiny, suffice it to say here that several of them have percolated down to textbooks widely used by undergraduate as well as postgraduate students in India and have thus sunk deep into the popular consciousness.

Through the long process of the evolution of an assertive Hindu identity several stereotypes about it have also crystallized. First, the Hindus were the autochthonous people of India and descendants of the Vedic Aryans and hence their religion was in existence in India right from the beginning and was eternal. Secondly, the eternal religion derived legitimacy from the Vedic corpus and hence was monolithic in character. Thirdly, the Hindus constituted a religious community separated historically from Muslims not only in terms of social customs and religious beliefs but also in their dietary culture so that the Muslims killed cows for food and the Hindus treated them as sacred and religiously abstained from eating beef. Fourth, Hinduism was the most tolerant religion in the world and hence there was no need for it to proselytize. But I propose to argue in the following pages that none of these stereotypes stands up to scrutiny in the light of historical evidence. The first essay questions the fantastic antiquity assigned to Hinduism and its supposed monolithic and eternal character. This is followed by an essay which examines the evidence of religious conflicts in early India and suggests that Hinduism, like all other religions, has been intolerant and that, contrary to popular belief, the adherents of its various sects fought among themselves a long time before the arrival of Islam and thus contests the misleading view that religious conflict was brought to India by its followers. The third and the last essay examines the sacred cow concept in the light of the Brāhmaṇical religious textual tradition and argues against the cliché that the practice of killing cows for food was introduced into India by Muslims and that abstention from eating beef is a mark of Hindu identity.

1 Deconstructing Hindu Identity

I

The quest for India's national identity through the route of Hindu religious nationalism began in the nineteenth century and has continued ever since. In recent years, however, it has received an unprecedented boost from those communal forces which brought a virulent version of Hindu cultural chauvinism to the centre stage of contemporary politics and produced a warped perception of India's past. This is evident from the indigenist propaganda writings which support the myth of Aryan autochthony, demonize Muslims and Christians, and propagate the idea that India and Hinduism are eternal. In an effort to prove the indigenous origin of Indian culture and civilization it has been argued, albeit vacuously, that the people who composed the Vedas called themselves Aryans and were the original inhabitants of India (Prinja 1996: 10; Guha 2005: 399). They are further described as the authors of the Harappan civilization, which the xenophobes and communalists insist on rechristening after the Vedic Saraswatī. Such views have received strong support from archaeologists whose writings abound in paralogisms (Gupta 1996; Lal 1998: 439–48);[1] and from their followers, whose works are dotted with fakes and frauds, a notable instance being the attempt to convert a Harappan "unicorn bull" into a Vedic horse so as to push the clock back on the date of the Vedas and thereby identify the Vedic people with the authors of the Harappan civilization.[2] This obsession with pushing back the chronology of Indian cultural traits and with denying the elements of change[3] has taken the form of a frenzied hunt for antiquity. We see a stubborn determination to "prove" that the Indian ("Hindu" is no different in the communal lexicon!) civilization is older than all others and was therefore free from any possible contamination in its early formative phase.

In this historiographical format India, i.e., Bhārata, is timeless. The first man was born here. Its people were the authors of the first human civilization, the Vedic, which is the same as the "Indus-Saraswatī." The authors of this civilization had reached the highest peak of achievement in all arts and sciences, and they were conscious of belonging to the Indian nation, which has existed eternally. This obsession with the antiquity of the Indian identity, civilization and nationalism has justifiably prompted several scholars, in recent years, to study and analyse the development of the idea of India (Mukherjee 2001; Habib 1999:

18–29; idem 2005; Ray 2004; Goswami 2004). Most of them have rightly argued that India as a country evolved over a long period, that the formation of its identity had much to do with the perceptions of the people who migrated into the subcontinent at different times, and that Indian nationalism developed mostly as a response to Western imperialism. But not all of them have succeeded in rising above the tendency to trace Indian national identity back to ancient times. For instance, a respected historian of ancient India tells us that "the inhabitants of the subcontinent were considered by the Purāṇic authors as forming a nation" and "could be called by a common name—Bhāratī" (Mukherjee 2001: 6; Ray 2004: 49, 55, nn. 33, 34). Assertions like this are very close to the Hindu jingoism which attributes all major modern cultural, scientific and political developments, including the idea of nationalism, to the ancient Indians. Although their detailed refutation may amount to a *rechauffe* of what has already been written on the historical development of the idea of India, I propose to argue against the fantastic antiquity assigned to Bhārata and Hinduism, as well as against the historically invalid stereotypes about the latter, and thus to show the lack of substance behind the ideas which have been the staple diet of the monster of Hindu cultural nationalism in recent years.

II

The geographical horizon of the early Aryans, as we know, was limited to the north-western part of the Indian subcontinent, referred to as Saptasindhava (*ṚV*, VIII, 24, 27)[4] and the word Bhārata in the sense of a country is absent from the entire Vedic literature, though the Bharata tribe is mentioned at several places in different contexts. In the *Aṣṭādhyāyī* (IV.2.113) of Pāṇini (500 BCE) we find a reference to Prācya Bharata in the sense of a territory (*janapada*) which lay between *Udīcya* (north) and *Prācya* (east). It must have been a small region occupied by the Bharatas and cannot be equated with the Akhaṇḍabhārata or Bhārata of the Hindutva camp. The earliest reference to Bhāratavarṣa (Prākrit Bharadhavasa) is found in the inscription of Khāravela (first century BCE) who lists it among the territories he invaded (Sircar 1965: no. 91, line 10), but it did not include Magadha, which is mentioned separately in the record. The word may refer here in a general way to northern India, but its precise territorial connotation is vague. A much larger geographical region is visualized by the use of the word in the *Mahābhārata* (composed over the period c. 200 BCE to 300 CE), which provides a good deal of geographical information about the subcontinent, although a large part of the Deccan and the far south does not find any place in it. Among the five divisions of Bhāratavarṣa named, Madhyadeśa finds frequent mention in ancient Indian texts; in the *Amarakośa* (also known as the *Nāmaliṅgānuśāsana*), a work of the fourth–fifth centuries, it is used synonymously with Bhārata and Āryāvarta (II.6,8); the latter, according to its eleventh-century commentator Kṣīrasvāmin, being the same as Manu's holy land situated between the Himalayas and the Vindhya range (II.22).[5] But in Bāṇa's *Kādambarī* (seventh century), at one place (1968: 290; Agrawal 1958: 188) Bhāratavarṣa is said to have been ruled by Tārāpīḍa, who "set his seal on the four oceans" (*dattacatuḥsamudramudraḥ*); and at another, Ujjainī is indicated as being outside Bhāratavarṣa (*Kādambarī* 1968: 311; Agrawal 1958: 205), which leaves its location far from clear. Similarly, in the *Nītivākyāmṛta* of Somadeva (tenth century), the word *bhāratīyāḥ* cannot be taken to mean anything more than the inhabitants of Bhārata, which itself remains undefined (*prakīrṇaka* 78).

Bhāratavarṣa figures prominently in the Purāṇas, but they describe its shape variously. In some passages it is likened to a half-moon, in others it is said to resemble a triangle; in yet others it appears as a rhomboid or an unequal quadrilateral or a drawn bow (Ali 1966: 109). The *Mārkaṇḍeya Purāṇa* compares the shape of the country with that of a tortoise floating on water and facing east (ibid.). Most of the Purāṇas describe Bhāratavarṣa as being divided into nine *dvīpas* or *khaṇḍas*, which, being separated by seas, were mutually inaccessible. The Purāṇic conception of Bhāratavarṣa has much correspondence with the ideas of ancient Indian astronomers like Varāhamihira (sixth century CE) and Bhāskarācārya (eleventh century). However, judging from their identifications of the rivers, mountains, regions and places mentioned in the Purāṇas, as well as from their rare references to areas south of the Vindhyas, their idea of Bhāratavarṣa does not seem to have included southern India. Although a few inscriptions of the tenth and eleventh centuries indicate that Kuntala (Karnataka) was situated in the land of Bhārata (Alam 2005: 43), which is described in a fourteenth-century record as extending from the Himalayas to the southern sea (*EI* XIV [1917–18], no. 3, lines 5-6), by and large the available textual and epigraphic references to it do not indicate that the term stood for India as we know it today.

An ambiguous notion of Bhārata is also found in the *Abhidhānacintāmaṇi* (IV.12; 1964: 235) of the Jain scholar Hemacandra (twelfth century), who describes it as the land of *karma* (*karmabhūmi*), as opposed to that of *phala* (*phalabhūmi*). Although he does not clarify what is meant by the two, his definition of Āryāvarta (which may correspond with Bhārata) is the same as that found in Manu (IV.14). In fact, Āryāvarta figures more frequently than Bhārata in the geohistorical discourses found in early Indian texts. It was only from the 1860s that the name Bhāratavarṣa, in the sense of the whole subcontinent, found its way into the popular vocabulary. Its visual evocation came perhaps not earlier than 1905 in a painting by Abanindranath Tagore, who conceived of the image as one of Bangamātā but later, "almost as an act of generosity towards the larger cause of Indian nationalism, decided to title it 'Bhāratmātā' " (Bose 1997: 53–54).[6] Thus it was only from the sixties and seventies of the nineteenth century that the notion of Bhārata was "forged by the self-conscious appropriation and transposition of discourse at once British-colonial, historical, geographical and ethnological, as well as received Puranic chronotopes" (Goswami 2004: chapters 5–6).

In many texts Bhārata is said to have been a part of Jambūdvīpa, which itself had an uncertain geographical connotation. The Vedic texts do not mention it; nor does Pāṇini, though he refers (IV.3.165) to the *jambū* (the rose apple tree). The early Buddhist canonical works provide the earliest reference to the continent called Jambūdvīpa (Jambūdīpa), its name being derived from the *jambū* tree which grew there, having a height of one hundred *yojanas*,[7] a trunk fifteen *yojanas* in girth and outspreading branches fifty *yojanas* in length, whose shade extended to one hundred *yojanas* (Malalasekera 1983: 941–42). It was one of the four *mahādīpas* (*mahādvīpas*) ruled by a Cakkavattī. We are told that Buddhas and Cakkavattīs were born only in Jambūdīpa, whose people were more courageous, mindful and religious than the inhabitants of Uttarakuru (Malalasekera 1983: 942). Going by the descriptions of Jambūdīpa and Uttarakuru in the early Buddhist literature, they both appear to be mythical regions. However, juxtaposed with Sihaladīpa (Siṃhaladvīpa = Sri Lanka), Jambūdīpa stands for India (*Mahāvaṃsa*, V.13; *Cūlavaṃsa*, XXXVII.216, 246; Malalasekera 1983: 942). Aśoka thus uses the word to mean the whole of his empire, which covered nearly the entire Indian subcontinent excluding the far southern part of its peninsula (Sircar 1965: no. 2, line 2).

Ambiguity about the territorial connotation of Jambūdvīpa continued during subsequent centuries in both epigraphic and literary sources. In a sixth-century inscription of Toramāṇa, for instance, Jambūdvīpa occurs without reference to any precise geographical region (Sircar 1965: no. 56, line 9). Similarly, the identification of Jambūdvīpa remains uncertain in the Purāṇic cosmological schema, where it appears more as a mythical region than as a geographical entity. The world, according to the Purāṇas, "consists of seven concentric dvīpas or islands, each of which is encircled by a sea, the central island called Jambūdvīpa" (Sircar 1960: 8–9). This is similar to the cosmological imaginings of the Jains who, however, placed Jambūdvīpa at the centre of the central land (*madhyaloka*) of the three-tiered structure of the universe (*Jaina Purāṇa Kośa* 1993: 256, 259).[8] According to another Purāṇic conception, which is similar to the Buddhist cosmological ideas, the earth is divided into four *mahādvīpas*, Jambūdvīpa being larger than the others (ibid: 9 n. 1). In both these conceptions of the world, Bhāratavarṣa is at some places said to be a part of Jambūdvīpa but at others the two are treated as identical (Sircar 1960: 6, 8).

Since these differently imagined geographical conceptions of Bhārata and Jambūdvīpa are factitious and of questionable value, to insist that their inhabitants formed a nation in ancient times is sophistry. It legitimates the Hindutva perception of Indian national identity as located in remote antiquity, accords centrality to the supposed primordiality of Hinduism and thus spawns Hindu cultural nationalism.[9] All this draws sustenance from, among other things, a systematic abuse of archaeology by a number of scholars, notably B. B. Lal. The *Pañcatantra* stories, he tells us, are narrated on the pots found in the digs at Lothal (Lal 1997: 175), and the people in Kalibangan cooked their food on clay *tandurs* which anticipated their use in modern times (Lal 2002: 95). The Harappans, his sciolism goes on, practised the modern "Hindu way of greeting" (*namaskāramudrā*); their women, like many married ones of our own times, applied vermillion (*sindūr*) in the partings of their hair and wore small and large bangles, identical to those in use nowadays, up to their upper arms. They are said to have practised fire worship (which is attested to by the Vedic texts and not by Harappan archaeology!) and to have worshipped *liṅga* and *yoni*, the later Śaivism being pushed back to Harappan times. An attempt is thus made to bolster an archaic and ill-founded view—supported and recently revived by several scholars[10]—that the Harappan religion, which, according to the Hindu cultural nationalists was in fact "Vedic-Hindu" was "the linear progenitor" of modern Hinduism (Gupta 1996: 147).

III

Those, including some supposed scholars, with an *idée fixe* about the incredible antiquity of the Indian nation and Hinduism have created several stereotypes about Hinduism over the years, especially recently, and these have percolated down to textbooks. A few sample statements from two books randomly picked from amongst a large number adequately illustrate the point: "Hinduism [is] a *very* old religion...sanatana dharma i.e. the Eternal Spiritual Tradition of India" (Lal *et al.* 2002: 133). "The Vedas are...recognised...as the most ancient literature in the world. The term 'sanatana' is often used to highlight this quality"

(Prinja 1996: 7).[11] "...freedom of thought and form of worship is unique to Hinduism" (Prinja 1996: 13). "In Hindu history no example of coercion or conversion can be found" (54). "...there is no conflict [in Hinduism] between science and religion" (153).

The above quotations contain several clichés which lend support to militant Hindu cultural nationalism. One of these—the imagined "oldness"—of what has come to be known as Hinduism—has been a parrot-cry of Hindu rightist groups and needs to be examined in the light of historical evidence. It is not necessary to go into the etymological peregrinations of the word "Hindu," derived from "Sindhu," on which much has been written; suffice it to say that the earliest use of the word, as is well known, can be traced back to the *Zend Avesta*, which speaks of Hapta Hindu (identical with the Ṛgvedic Saptasindhava) as one of the sixteen regions created by Ahur Mazda. The word retained its territorial connotation for a long time and did not acquire any religious dimension. According to one scholar (Sharma 2002: 3–4), the earliest use of the word "Hindu" in a religious sense is found in the account of Hsüan Tsang (Beal 1981: 69), who tells us that the bright light of "holy men and sages, guiding the world as the shining of the moon, have made this country eminent and so it is called In-tu"—the Chinese name for India being Indu, moon. But the religious affiliation, if any, of these "holy men and sages" remains unknown, which hardly supports the view that Hsüan Tsang used the word In-tu (Hindu) in a specifically religious sense: indeed, the later Chinese pilgrim I-tsing questioned the veracity of the statement that it was a common name for the country (Takakusu 1966: 118).

Similarly, the suggestion that the use of the word "Hindu" in a religious sense began immediately after the conquest of Sind by Muḥammad ibn Qāsim in 712 is hardly tenable. It has been asserted that the "Hindu" was "now identified on a religious basis" and that "conversion from this Hindu religion" was now possible.[12] The sources bearing on eighth-century Sind indicate the existence of several non-Islamic religions and sects of Brāhmaṇism and Buddhism denoted by the Arabic compound *barhimah-samaniyah* used by the classical Muslim writers,[13] but the word "Hindu" in their writings had a geographic, linguistic, or ethnic connotation. In the *Chachnāma*, for example, *hinduvān* means Indians in general and *hindavī* stands for the Indian language (Maclean 1989: 12–13; Habib 1994: 8–9). The term "Hindu" continued to have several meanings in subsequent times. The classical Persian poets used the word in various senses—the black complexion of the Indian, the beloved's tresses, a mole on the cheek, or the planet Saturn—to describe anything black (Ernst 2004: 23). "Hindu" also indicated slavery in contradistinction to the Turkish rulership but Sultān Mahmūd's protégé

Firdausī in his *Shāhnāma* portrayed Alexander the Great as addressing a letter to an Indian ruler with the salutation "Best of the Hindus, wise, knowing, and clear minded" (Ernst 2004: 23). The wide range of connotations of the term in classical Persian literature thus presents a conundrum, though Alberuni, another protégé of Sultan Mahmud, is widely believed to have mentioned it as a religious designation in his *Kitāb-al-Hind* written in Arabic (1030 CE).

Alberuni (973–1048) was born in Khwarezm from where he was brought as prisoner of war by Sultān Mahmūd of Ghazna, who subsequently became his patron. He learnt Sanskrit language and acquired a good knowledge of Indian religious as well as scientific texts. Not surprisingly his is arguably the first comprehensive description of the religions of India. But his purpose was not to define Hinduism; for going by the available translation of his Arabic text, it appears that at one place he distinguishes Hindus(?) from Buddhists but at another holds the distinction to be between śramans (Buddhists) and brāhmaṇs (Sachau 1910: 7, 21; Habib 2005: 5 n. 14). He states that "they (Hindus?) totally differ from us in religion" (Sachau 1910: 19) and, on the basis of his knowledge of Sanskrit, describes the differences between Islamic and the Indian cultures in terms of language, Indian xenophobia, customs, and philosophical thought, religious beliefs and practices.

Giving an account of the nature of God, with reference to his speech, knowledge and action (Sachau 1910: 27–30) Alberuni makes a distinction between the ideas of the elite and those of the common people (Sachau 1910: 31–32). He points out that the elite or "those who march on the path to liberation or study philosophy and theology, and desire truth" worship God (Sachau 1910: 113) and the uneducated common people—"even those who adhered to Judaism, Christianity and Islam, need concrete objects of worship" and hence practised idolatry (Friedmann 1975: 215).[14] His treatment of the religious views of the elite and the idolatrous practices of the common people give the impression that his understanding was limited largely to Brāhmaṇical religious beliefs and practices. In spite of this, the "remarkable clarity" of his perception of the "otherness of the Indian religious philosophical context and horizon" remains indubitable, but to say that it was "effectively the invention of the concept of a unitary Hindu religion…" is unlikely to meet general acceptance. Several scholars[15] have, in fact, asserted that Alberuni did not use the word "Hindu" at all in his text, in either the religious or ethnic sense. The nineteenth-century English translator, according to them, "liberally uses the word Hindu," whereas "the original Arabic text appears only to use phrases literally equivalent to 'of the people of India'" (Lorenzen 2006: 34; Alatas 2008: 16). It will be therefore too much to assume that Alberuni presented a clear and coherent understanding of a unitary Hindu religion[16] or to credit him with any definite and essentialist view[17] of it and treat his perception as a landmark in the development of Hindu religious identity.

The ambivalence surrounding the word "Hindu" continued for a long time, so that even three centuries after Alberuni we find Ziyāud-dīn Baranī, the first Muslim to write the history of India (known as the *Tārīkh-i-Fīrūzshāhī*), making as many as forty references to Hindus (Hunūd and Hindu'ān) either as a religious category or as a political one and sometimes as both (Ahmad 1982: 295–302),[18] describing them as "worshippers of idols and cowdung" and advocating stringent action against them (Friedman 1975: 214–15).

In the sixteenth century, despite Akbar's familiarity with and patronage of non-Islamic religions of India, Abū-l Faẓl could do no better than "merely give resumes of Brahmanism...presumably because this was the most prestigious" (Thapar 1997: 73), and these are nowhere near the notion of a Hindu religion. Half a century after his death, the anonymous author[19] of the *Dabistān-i-Mazāhib*, who claimed to present a survey of all religions and sects, devoted one full chapter to the religion of the Hindus and other Indian sects but failed to provide a clear understanding of what was intended by the use of the term "Hindu." In his work, the word means the orthodox Brāhmaṇical groups ("smartians") as well as the non-Islamic belief systems of various schools, sects, castes and religions of India. At some places the rubric "Hindu" includes Jains and at others it excludes them, along with the Yogīs, Sanyāsīs, Tapasīs and Cārvakas (Mishra 2003). A similar vagueness in the connotation of the word is seen more than a hundred years later in the history of Gujarat called the *Mirāt-i-Ahmadī*, authored by 'Alī Muḥammad Khān (1761), who uses it "as a term of reference for people of all religions, castes, sub-castes, and professions who can be classified as a group different from the Muslims" and "reckons the Jain clergy (Shevra) and the laity (Shravak) as Hindus even though he is aware of the difference in the religious persuasions of, as well as the antagonism between, the Jains and the Vaishnavites (Maishris)" (Haider 2005). The fuzziness of definitions of "Hindu" and "Hinduism" is thus unquestionable. This is rooted, to a large extent, in the fact that Arabic and Persian scholarship describes all non-Muslim Indians as Hindus.

What possibly added to the ambiguity surrounding the word is the fact that no Indians described themselves as Hindus before the fourteenth century. The earliest use of the word in the Sanskrit language occurs in a 1352 inscription of Bukka, the second ruler of Vijayanagara's first dynasty, who described himself with a series of titles, one of them being *hindurāya suratrāṇa* (Sultan among Hindu kings). His successors continued to use this title for 250 years, "until as late as the opening years of the seventeenth century" (Wagoner 1996: 862; cf. Kulke 1993: 208–39). In north India, Rāṇā Kumbha was the first to style himself as *hindusuratrāṇa* in an inscription dated 1439 (Chattopadhyaya 1998: 54). Despite the use of the title by royalty, the word "Hindu" does not occur in mainstream Sanskrit literature until the early nineteenth century, with the rare exceptions of Jonarāja's *Rājataraṅgiṇī* (1455–59), which uses the word as part of the compound *hindughoṣa*[20] perhaps to mean the Hindukush mountain (verse 381), and Śrīvara's *Jaina Rājataraṅgiṇī* (1459–77), which refers to the social customs of the Hindus (*hindukasamācāra*, 3.218) and their language (*hindsthānavācā*, 2.215) as distinct from the Persian language (*pārasībhāsayā*) and also mentions (2.51) a place called Hinduvāḍā (modern Hindubata, 15 miles north of Sopore). The three Sanskrit texts of the Gauḍīya Vaiṣṇava tradition, ranging from the early sixteenth to the late eighteenth centuries, do not mention the word "Hindu" at all (O'Connell 1973: 340–43); nor does it occur in the *Brahmasūtra* commentary written by the famous Gauḍīya Vaiṣṇava *ācārya* Baladeva Vidyābhūṣaṇa (1750), who tried to "affiliate the Krishna Chaitanya tradition with 'official' Advaita Vedānta" (Halbfass 1990: 193). It is not until the first half of the nineteenth century that the word "Hindu" begins to appear in the Sanskrit texts produced as a result of Christianity's encounters with Brāhmaṇical religion. Among the religious debates and disputations of the early nineteenth century centring round the alleged superiority of Christianity vis-à-vis Brāhmaṇism, an important controversy was generated by John Muir's evangelist critique published as *Mataparīkṣā* (in Sanskrit) in 1839, which provoked three Indian pandits to defend their religion.[21] One of them, Haracandra Tarkapancānana (1940: 1; Young 1981: 93), in his reply to Muir, impugned him as *hindudharmātivairin* (Hinduism's great foe) and laid down conditions for becoming "eligible" [*adhikārin*] for [Vedic] *dharma*, "having become Hindus [*hindutvam prāpya*] in a subsequent birth" (Young 1981: 150). But the occurrence of the word "Hindu" in Sanskrit texts remained rare, and the two nineteenth-century Bengali encyclopaedists, Rādhākānta Deb (1783–1867) and Tārānātha Tarkavācaspati (1811–85)[22] could not cite any text other than the obscure and very late *Merutantra* (eighteenth century),[23] providing an extremely specious etymology of the word[24] based on it.

The word "Hindu" is rarely seen in the mediaeval vernacular *bhakti* literature as well. Ten Gauḍīya Vaiṣṇava texts in Bengali, ranging in dates from the sixteenth to the eighteenth centuries, were examined. The word "Hindu" was found forty-one times, and *Hindudharma* seven times, in the 80,000 couplets of only five of the ten texts. Apart from the small number of occurrences, the interesting aspect of the evidence is that there is no explicit discussion of what "Hindu" or *Hindudharma* means (O'Connell

1973). The word "Hindu" is also used in different contexts by Vidyāpati (early fifteenth century), Kabīr (1450–1520), Ekanāth (1533–99) and Anantadās (sixteenth century). On this basis a scholar has argued that a Hindu religious identity defined itself primarily in opposition to Muslims and Islam and had a continuous existence through the mediaeval period[25]—a view remarkably close to that articulated by the communalist historians. This argument is deeply flawed because it is based on the patently wrong assumption that all non-Muslims were part of the postulated Hindu identity and ignores the basic fact that the mediaeval *sants* and *bhakti* poets used the term "Hindu" with reference to adherents of the caste-centric Brāhmaṇical religion, against which they raised their voice (Bahuguna 2003a, 2003b; cf. idem 1999). The general absence of the words "Hindu" and "*Hindudharma*" in the precolonial Sanskrit texts and their limited connotation in the not-too-frequent occurrences in the *bhakti* literature clearly indicate that Indians did not create a Hindu religious identity for themselves, as is argued by some. Of course the word was in use in precolonial India, but it was not before the late eighteenth or early nineteenth centuries that it was appropriated by Western, especially British, scholars[26] whose writings helped the imperial administration to formulate and create the notion of Hinduism in the sense in which we understand it today. The British borrowed the word "Hindu" from India, gave it a new meaning and significance, reimported it into India as a reified phenomenon called Hinduism,[27] and used it in censuses and gazetteers as a category in their classification of the Indian people, paving the way for the global Hindu religious identity—a process perceptively equated with the "pizza effect," based on how the Neapolitan hot baked bread exported to America returned with all its embellishments to Italy to become its national dish (Bharati 1970: 267–87). Given this background, Hinduism was a creation of the colonial period and cannot lay claim to any great antiquity.[28] Although some echo the views of B. B. Lal and his followers to proclaim that its origins lay in the Indus valley civilization and in what they call Aryan culture (Flood 2004: 50), Hinduism may yet be held to be the youngest of all religions, a nineteenth-century neologism popularized by the British (Davis 1998a: 5; Hawley 1991: 20–23; Doniger 1991: 35–41). That it has come to stay, despite its endless ambiguities of connotation,[29] is a different matter.

IV

Just as Hinduism as a religious category acquired much visibility in Christian missionary writings and in British administrative records (Cohn 1987: 224–54), so also it was not until the nineteenth century that it came to be labelled *sanātanadharma*. The term can be translated in a variety of ways: "eternal religion" or "eternal law" (Klostermaier 1990: 31, 530), "unshakeable, venerable order" (Halbfass 1990: 344), "ancient and continuing guideline" (Lipner 1994: 221) or "the eternal order or way of life" (Lipner 2005: 19). It has been used by a variety of representatives of modern Hinduism, ranging from neo-Hindus such as Vivekananda and Radhakrishnan to the leaders and followers of reform movements as well as their opponents. Although some scholars have tried to project it as having a "dynamic character," *sanātanadharma* was basically an orthodox resistance to reform movements[30] (Zavos 2001: 109–23; Dalmia 1997: 2–4 n. 5) and drew on references to itself in ancient Indian literature.

The earliest occurrence of the term is found in the two Buddhist canonical works, the *Suttanipāta* (453) and the *Dhammapada* (I.5). According to the former, "truth indeed is the undying word" (*saccaṃ ve amatā vācā esa dhammo sanātano*) and according to the latter the eternal law (*esa dhamma sanātano*)[31] is that hatred and enmities cease through love alone. But the expression *sanātanadharma* is mentioned frequently in the Brāhmaṇical texts as well. The *Mahābhārata* often uses the expression *eṣa dharmaḥ sanātanaḥ* "as a sanctioning formula intended to emphasise the obligatory nature of social and religious rules,"[32] but its use to justify Śvetaketu's mother's being snatched away by a brāhmaṇ would be far from palatable to modern sanātanists.[33] The *Gītā* (I.40) uses the term in the plural to mean the "venerable norms for the families" (*kuladharmāḥ sanātanāḥ*) and describes (XI.18) Kṛṣṇa as "protector of the established norms" (*śāśvatadharmagoptā sanātanaḥ*). Similarly, in the law book of Manu, *sanātanadharma* stands for established "customs and statutes of the countries, castes and families" (I.118; VII.98; IX.64, 325), though the Purāṇas use the term in various senses. According to the *Matsyapurāṇa* (143. 32; cf. *Brahmāṇḍapurāṇa* II.31.36-38; 91.30-32) it is rooted in virtues like the absence of greed and attachment, the practice of celibacy, forgiveness, compassion for living beings, and so on. The *Varāhapurāṇa* at one place refers to the eternal *dharma* promulgated by Varāha (126.7), and at another (126.43) states that according to the eternal law one should not sink into grief on seeing the fortunes of others and one's own distress (*eṣa dharmaḥ sanātanaḥ*). In the *Śivapurāṇa* (7.2.10.30-72), Śiva defines his eternal *dharma* (*dharmaḥ sanātanaḥ*) as consisting of *jñāna*, *kriyā*, *caryā* and *yoga*, though in several epic and Purāṇic passages *sanātana* is used as an epithet for divinities like Kṛṣṇa, or for Dharma, who himself is thought of as a deity. The *Uttararāmacarita* of Bhavabhūti (eighth century), the earliest secular work to refer to *sanātanadharma*, mentions it in the sense of fixed laws and customs; and the Khanapur plates (sixth century), which contain the earliest epigraphic reference to it, use it in speaking of rites and rituals prescribed by *śruti* and *smṛti* (*śrutismṛtivihitasanātanadharmakarmaniratāya*). Although these textual references provide different connotations of the term *sanātanadharma*, it has generally been understood in the sense of traditionally established customs and duties of countries, castes and families in texts as late as the *Mahānirvāṇatantra* (eighteenth century), by an unknown author, and the *Śāstratattvavinirṇaya* (1844) of Nilakaṇṭha (Nehemia) Goreh.

It was in the nineteenth century that *sanātanadharma* at last emerged as a key concept in traditionalist self-assertion against Christianity as well as in the reform movements (Brahmosamaj and Aryasamaj); it came to be stereotyped as a venerable, "eternal," "all encompassing" and "inclusive" (*sarvavyāpaka*) religion, "with no temporal beginning, no historical founding figure," one which needed no innovations or reforms (Halbfass 1990: 343). This added to the conceptual opacity and vagueness of the "timeless religion," which had to wait for its first codification by the English woman Annie Besant who, in collaboration with Indian scholars such as Bhagwan Das, drew up a textbook[34] on *sanātanadharma* for use at the Central Hindu College, Benares, whose establishment in 1898 owed much to her initiative.

V

Hinduism has often been viewed not only as eternal (*sanātanadharma*) but also as a monolithic religion in which there is "agreement about some static universal doctrine" (Lipner 1994: 221). This stereotype has received support not only from Hindu right-wing political groups but also from serious scholars of religion who define Hinduism as "the religion of those humans who create, perpetuate, and transform traditions with legitimizing reference to the authority of the Vedas" (Smith 1989: 13–14). An early, though indirect, endorsement of the legitimizing authority of the Vedas comes from Yāska (fifth century BCE), who describes Vedic "seers" as "having attained a direct experience of *dharma*" (*sākṣātkṛtadharma*, *Nirukta* I.20). Later, Manu (II.6; cf XII.95-96) categorically states that "the root of religion is the entire Veda" (*vedo'khilo dharmamūlam*), and that (II.10) the authority of the *śruti* and the *smṛti* is not to be questioned or reasoned about (*amimāṃsya*). His assertion has received much support over time from the different philosophical systems, though their apologetic patterns have varied considerably. Nyāya and Vaiśeṣika, though not affiliated to the Veda, recognized it as a "source of knowledge" (*pramāṇa*), and their leading early mediaeval thinkers—Uddyotakara, Vācaspatimiśra and Udayana—defended it, sometimes even by developing new arguments (Halbfass 1991: 24–27). Much stronger support for the Vedic texts, however, came from the Mimāṃsā, whose "genuine affiliation with, and commitment to, the Veda are generally accepted" (Halbfass 1991: 33). Mimāṃsā thinkers such as Kumārila, Prabhākara and Maṇḍanamiśra—all from the eighth century—laid great emphasis on the principle that the *dharma* is justified by the Veda alone (*vedamūlatva*) (Smith 1989: 18; Halbfass 1990: 326–29, 359; Renou 1965: 40–46). Similarly, Śaṅkara (eighth century) treated all the declarations of the Veda as authoritative (Renou 1965: 37) and defiance of it as *vedavirodha* or as heresy (Smith 1989: 18). Indeed, the acceptance of the authority of the Vedas is an important feature of Brāhmaṇical orthodoxy, but their number being only four, an amorphous category of the "fifth Veda" came into being leading to an open-endedness in the Vedic corpus, a phenomenon also in keeping with the general absence of and aversion to writing and the Brāhmaṇical preference for the oral transmission of all knowledge (Staal 1979: 121–24; cf. Mackenzie Brown 1986: 68–86).

The notion of a "fifth Veda" is found as early as the later Vedic period when the *Chandogya Upaniṣad* (7.2; 1991: 470) declares legends and ancient lore to be the fifth Veda (*itihāsapurāṇaṃ pañcamaṃ vedānāṃ vedam*). Not surprisingly, the *Atharvaveda*, which according to some scholars, did not originally belong to the "revealed" Vedic corpus, earned the status of a "divine revelation" only when its followers invented legends and allegories to prove the superiority of the text (Sarup 1984: 72–73). In subsequent times many genres of Indian religious literature were equated with the Vedas. The *Mahābhārata* explicitly claims (1.57.74ab; Brockington 1998: 7) the status of the "fifth Veda" (*vedān adhāpayām āsa mahābhāratapañcamān*) and subsumes all knowledge and traditions and declares (I.56.33) that "that which is found herein exists elsewhere; that which is not here, is nowhere" (*yad ihāsti tad anyatra, yan nehāsti na tat kvacid*). The Purāṇas often claim to be essence of all the Vedas (*sarvavedasāra, akhilaśrutisāra, sarvavedārthasāra*), or the soul (*ātman*) of the Vedas[35] (Smith 1989: 26); the *Bhāgavatapurāṇa* (I.4.20) even describes itself as the fifth Veda or the Veda of the Kaliyuga and the later Vaiṣṇava schools called it the *Viṣṇuveda*. Some Tantras also acknowledge the Vedas (Flood 2003: 2080); the *Kulārṇavatantra*, for instance, states that the *kuladharma* was "churned by Śiva with the churning-stick of wisdom" (Goudriaan and Gupta 1981: 19). Similarly, the large body of Tamil Śaiva and Vaiṣṇava devotional hymns, ranging in date from the sixth to the ninth centuries CE, claimed Vedic status despite their unvedic/antivedic thrust. This is evident from the fact that Nammāḷvār's *Tiruvāymoḷi* was described as *Draviḍaveda*. The tradition of extending the use of the word Veda appears particularly strong in southern India where even the Christian missionaries used it to describe their Bible (Halbfass 1990: 340).[36] Many religious teachers holding different opinions sought to legitimize their teachings with reference to the Vedas during the mediaeval period. Acceptance of the authority of the Vedas is in fact an important feature even of modern Hindu revivalist movements such as the Arya Samaj of Dayananda, who is sometimes called the Luther of India (Jordens 1978; Llewellyn 1993). But all this cannot be construed to mean that Hinduism acquired a monolithic character: for it has rightly been pointed out that allegiance to the Vedas was very often a fiction, nothing more than a mere "raising of the hat, in passing, to an idol by which one no longer intends to be encumbered later on" (Renou 1965: 2).

There is substantial evidence to show that the Vedas did not always enjoy a pre-eminent position even in Brāhmaṇical Hinduism.[37] Anti-Vedic ideas, in fact, began to find expression in the *Ṛgveda* itself. The famous Ṛgvedic passage (VII.103) which equated brāhmaṇs with croaking frogs was an early attempt to ridicule the Vedas and their reciters. In addition to the satirization of the brāhmaṇs, there is also evidence of the questioning of Vedic knowledge: "Whence this creation developed is known only by him who witnesses this world in the highest heaven—or perhaps even he does not know" (X.129.7). At several places in the *Ṛgveda*, Indra is abused and his very existence is questioned (Heesterman 1985: 77), though he appears in this text as the most important god to whom the largest number of hymns, some two hundred and fifty of them, are addressed. Thus in a hymn to Indra it is said: "to Indra, if Indra exists" (VIII.100.3), and in another the question is asked (II.12.5): "about whom they ask, where is he? ... And they say about him, 'he is not'..." (II.12). Scepticism about the Vedic sacrifice was expressed by reviling it at the end of the *mahāvrata* Soma festival, as is evident from several Ṛgvedic passages (Heesterman 1985: 75; Doniger 1971: 284 n. 83).[38] The sanctity of the Vedas was questioned soon after their composition as can be inferred from a number of later Vedic texts. The Upaniṣads contain several passages which deprecate the Vedas. The *Muṇḍaka Upaniṣad* (I.1.4-5), for example, regards the four Vedas as "lower knowledge" (*aparāvidyā*).[39] Similarly, in the *Nirukta*, Yāska (sixth–fifth centuries BCE) describes Kautsa as saying that "the Vedic stanzas have no meaning" and that "their meaning is contradictory" (Sarup 1984: I.15). Indications of the undermining of Vedic rituals are also found in the Dharmaśāstra texts, which have been the main vehicle of Vedic thought. Baudhāyana, for instance, cites the view that "non-Vedic local practices may be allowed in their own territory," though his own opinion is that "one must never follow practices opposed to the tradition of learned authorities" (Doniger 1971: 286).

An unwillingness to concede a legitimizing role to the Veda manifested itself in many texts representing the various strands of Brāhmaṇical thought. For example, in the *Gītā*, which has been the most popular Hindu religious text through the centuries, Kṛṣṇa tells (II.41-46) Arjuna in unambiguous terms that those who delight in the eulogistic statements of the Vedas (*vedavādaratāḥ*) are full of worldly desires (*kāmātmānaḥ*), and that the desire-ridden followers (*kāmakāmāḥ*) of the Vedic sacrificial rites stagnate in the world (IX.21; cf XI.48, 53). The Purāṇas often undermine the supremacy of the Vedas despite their general allegiance to them. While some of them (*Matsyapurāṇa*, 53.3.20, 5.3.1.20) tell us that God thought of the Purāṇas before he spoke the Vedas, others (*Nāradīyapurāṇa*, 2.24.16) state that the Vedas are "established" on the Purāṇas (Smith 1989: 26). "There is no higher essence or truth than this," the *Agnipurāṇa* tells us, and "there is no better book, ...there is no better *śāstra*, or *śruti* or...*smṛti*...for this Purāṇa is supreme" (383, 47–50; Brown 1986: 70–71). The *Bhāgavatapurāṇa* was similarly said to have superseded and transcended the Vedas; its authors even claim that the Veda itself was created by Viṣṇu and thus relegate it to a secondary place. Jīva Goswāmī (sixteenth century) of the Gauḍīya Vaiṣṇava school vehemently denied that this text was based on the Vedas at all (Halbfass 1990: 366). Despite the fact that the authors of the Tāntric texts tried to base their doctrines on the Vedas, they also undermined the Vedic authority. For example, the *Kulārṇavatantra*, a mediaeval text, has contempt for the six schools of philosophy and all kinds of textual traditions and, in contrast to its assertion regarding the origin of the *kuladharma* (*supra*), even goes to the extent of asserting that the Vedas, Purāṇas and Śāstras display themselves like prostitutes. Similarly the *Mahānirvāṇatantra*, an eighteenth-century work, states that the Vedas, Purāṇas and Śāstras are of no use in the *kaliyuga* (Urban 2001: 105; Granoff 1991–92: 287; White 2003: 152; Bhattacharyya 1982: 75) and "declares that all of the other religious traditions are encompassed by and disappear within the Tantric *kuladharma*, just as the tracks of all other animals disappear within the tracks of the elephant" (Halbfass 1990: 366).[40] All this may not amount to a repudiation of the Vedas, but it certainly indicates that all post-Vedic Brāhmaṇical religious traditions did not look to them for legitimacy.

Several religious movements within the fold of what is now known as Hinduism in fact rejected the authority of both the brāhmaṇs and the Vedas. Vīraśaivism, a Śaivite sect whose followers are also called Liṅgāyats and which gained prominence in Karnataka in the twelfth century, is a case in point. Its hagiographical texts bear ample testimony to the fact that, at least in the early phase, the Vīraśaivas ridiculed the Vedas and unequivocally rejected them. The *Bāsavapurāṇa* speaks of a Vedāntist who was humiliated by Bāsava at the court of Bijjala, and the *Cennabāsavapurāṇa* narrates how a Vedic scholar was ridiculed by the Liṅgāyats, who had the Vedas recited by dogs (Nandi 2000: 485 n. 47).[41] Similarly, the adherents of the south Indian Śrī-vaiṣṇava sect of Tenkalai rejected the Vedas and composed their own Veda, called the *Nālāyiraprabandham* (Renou 1965: 2). This rejection of Vedic authority seems to have been a feature of other mediaeval religious movements as well. The Mahānubhāvas in Maharashtra and the Sahajiyās in Bengal also renounced the Vedas. So did individual mediaeval *bhakti* saints like Kabīr (fifteenth–sixteenth centuries), Tukārām (seventeenth century), and several others. As recently as the nineteenth century, precisely at the time when Dayananda Saraswati was busy spreading the word that the Vedas are the repository of all knowledge, they were rejected by Ramakrishna, who said: "the truth is not in the Vedas; one should act according to the Tantras, not according to the Vedas, the latter are impure from the very fact of their being pronounced" (Renou 1965: 3). Evidently, thus, different religious sects have not had the same attitude towards the Vedic corpus, and even the texts of specific sectarian affiliations often express contradictory views about it. This being so, the stereotype of a monolithic Hinduism based on the Vedas must be seen as a myth deliberately propagated by some scholars as well as by right-wing Hindu groups, all of whom not only ignore the plurality of religious beliefs and practices covered by the umbrella term "Hinduism," invented in the colonial period, but who also deny the centuries-long process of their evolution.

VI

The stereotyping of Hinduism as eternal, monolithic, tolerant and non-proselytizing began soon after its invention in the nineteenth century, and the effort to present it as different from all the other religions of the world has gathered momentum over the years. Not content with imagining their religion to be unique, the Hindu cultural nationalists persist in noisily proclaiming its imagined uniqueness. The clichés about it receive inspiration and support from the writings of "scholars of religion" based at universities in the West, where departments of religious studies or comparative religion have mushroomed after World War II, their number having come to exceed 1,200 in the U.S. alone (Kwangsu Lee 2003: 28). Most of the scholars affiliated to these departments and a few of their Indian disciples are inspired by Joachim Wach and Mircea Eliade (Lee 2003: 28) and speak of the science of religion (*religionswis-*

senschaft): but in reality they study Hinduism as a socio-historically autonomous phenomenon, thus supporting the claim that religion is *sui generis*.[42] Opposed to the scientific analysis of religious data and to any kind of reductionism, they have studied religion by prioritizing "interior and generally inaccessible personal experiences and religious convictions at the expense of observable and documentable data" (McCutcheon 2003: 128), focusing on the "transhistorical religious meaning of any given hierophany" (Lee 2003: 12–13). The influence of these scholars is reflected in the anti-historical attitude of the bulk of writing on Hinduism produced by Western scholars and their Indian followers. For example, one of the leading Western scholars of religion, and possibly the most influential, Wendy Doniger, has studied many neglected aspects of Hinduism (e.g., myths, symbols, metaphors) on the basis of an extensive use of Sanskrit texts and has provided interesting and provocative interpretations of the early Indian myths and religions, bravely facing the Hindu diaspora's wrath. But she has generally shied away from examining their changing social contexts. The same may be said of several recent publications on Hinduism which do not view religion as a multifactoral historical and cultural process but as a decontextualized phenomenon not linked to material realities on the ground.[43]

There are a few exceptions from India,[44] but most Western scholars writing on various aspects of early Indian religions, especially Hinduism, describe them merely as systems of faith and salvation and "prioritize their abstract essences and homogeneity over their socio-political context" (McCutcheon 2003: 3). In their works, phenomenology takes precedence over rational historical enquiry and a subtle defence of Hinduism masquerades as serious academic enterprise. Naturally, stereotypes about it tend to become deep-rooted and their grip on the masses strong.

The study of religion in academia needs to be rescued from those "scholars of religion" who accept premises that strengthen the stereotypes which feed religious fundamentalism and who unnecessarily take upon themselves the task of defending "the religiosity of religion," a task which the sybaritic sadhus, despite their questionable personal track records, can discharge with greater efficiency. Historians cannot be the custodians of religion: their task is to critically examine it.

2 Tolerant Hinduism: Evidence and Stereotype

I

It is proclaimed often and loudly that, unlike Christianity and Islam, Hinduism is a tolerant and non-proselytizing religion. Although this idea is peddled perpetually by the Hindu Right and receives an easy popular acceptance, it is rooted, to a significant extent, in the European writings on India. Half a millennium after Alberuni referred to the Indian xenophobia, a French doctor, François Bernier by name, who travelled widely in India during the 1660s, was one of the early Europeans to perceive Hindus as a tolerant people and to state that they "did not claim that their law is universal" (Halbfass 1990: 407). Similarly Herder (1744–1803), the forerunner of the Romantic glorification of India, referred to the Hindus as "mild" and "tolerant" and as "the gentlest branch of humanity"; and Immanuel Kant (1724–1804) said that they "do not hate the other religions but they believe they are also right." Such views find a more prominent place in the writings of Orientalists such as William Jones, according to whom "the Hindus...would readily admit the truth of the Gospel but they contend that it is perfectly consistent with their Sastras" (Marshall 1970: 245). In the nineteenth century, religious reformers emphasized the idea of tolerance in Hinduism. For example, Vivekananda (1863–1904) picked up the famous Ṛgvedic passage *ekaṃsad viprā vahudhā vadanti* to support his vision that "India alone [was] to be...the land of toleration"—a vision which, in reality, did not conform to his view that "all creeds may be equal but Hinduism [was] more equal" and to his projection of Hinduism as a "standard by which to measure both the theological and philosophical content as well as the histories of the other religions" (Brekke 2002: 40–42). The Ṛgvedic quote, which has been "milked for all its worth" since the time of Vivekananda, has become a cliché, and his prophecy itself, if seriously meant, has repeatedly been shown to be ill-founded.

Even so, the supposed tolerant nature of Hinduism has been the subject of considerable debate in academic circles in the twentieth century. Paul Hacker, for example, used the word "inclusivism" in his discussion of tolerance/intolerance in Indian religions and considered it exclusively an Indian phenomenon (Hacker 1957: 167–79). He has received considerable support from several scholars, the most recent being Brian Hatcher according to whom "eclecticism is an integral part of the Indian cultural tradition" (1999: 73, 86–88), though according to some scholars the modern concepts of religious toleration and freedom are the offspring of European civilization (Zagorin 2003: xii–xiii). Several scholars such as J. W. Hauer (1961: 90ff.) and Karl-Heinz Golzio (1990: 89–102) have, not surprisingly, questioned his views—the latter, in fact, refers to the statement of the Dvaita philosopher Madhva (1199–1278) according to whom the king should punish those who are against the Vaiṣṇavas (Golzio 1990: 92). During the period of the Indian freedom struggle the imagined inclusive and tolerant nature of Hinduism was emphasized by many leaders. Bal Gangadhar Tilak (1856–1920), despite his espousal of militant Hinduism, quite often cited the above Ṛgvedic passage to lay stress on religious tolerance (Sathe 1994: 114). Mohandas Karamchand Gandhi, who lived and died for religious harmony in India, found Hinduism to be the most tolerant of all religions known to him, though by taking pride in its inclusivism he made it exclusive (Misra 2004: 66–67)—a position similar to that of the greatest modern Indian philosopher S. Radhakrishnan (Minor 1982: 275–90). Jawaharlal Nehru, who is rightly considered to be the architect of a secular state in modern India, asserted that Hinduism's "essential spirit seems to be to live and let live" (1946: 75). The perception of Hinduism as a tolerant religion has predictably elicited conflicting responses from the scholarly community. On the one hand are scholars like the late Nirad C. Chaudhuri (1965: 39), who almost ruled out the idea of religious tolerance and asserted that "if the familiar words about the tolerance and capacity for synthesis were true, one would be hard put to it to explain why there are such deep suspicions and enmities among the human groups in India." On the other hand, there are many historians and social scientists who have emphasized the inclusive character of Hinduism. The influential literature generated by them in recent years, most notably by Amartya Sen (2005: 3–33), has glorified religious tolerance and inclusiveness in early India.

It is true that religious sects in early India, especially in the early mediaeval period, showed a certain degree of mutual accommodation, and one may offer several examples to illustrate this process. Thus, judging from the Purāṇic evidence, much of which belongs to the early mediaeval or even the later period, the Buddha, founder of a heretic religion, emerged as an *avatāra* of Viṣṇu around the middle of the sixth century CE (Hazra 1975: 41–42; Doniger 1988: 204–11) and figured as such not only in several Purāṇas[1] but also in many other sources including the *Daśāvatāracarita* of Kṣemendra and *Gītagovinda* of Jayadeva (Hazra 1975: 41; Chakrabarti 2001: 153) as well as inscriptions (Satri 1946; 1991: 5ff.) and, interestingly, in Alberuni's *Kitāb-al-Hind* (Sachau 1910: 380). Similarly, Ādinātha (Ṛṣabha), the first *tīrthaṅkara* of another heretic religion, Jainism, was accepted as an incarnation of Viṣṇu in the *Bhāgavatapurāṇa* (Jaini 2000: 325–49). Although sacrifice to the Buddha was recommended for worshippers desirous of beauty (*rūpakāmo yajed buddhaṃ, Varāhapurāṇa*, 48.22) and a way was thus opened for brāhmaṇ priests to officiate at Buddhist temples (Jaini 2001: 90), it is forgotten that Śiva is believed to have appeared on earth in the form of Śaṅkara to combat the Buddha *avatāra* just as it is suppressed that Nārāyaṇācārya described Śaṅkara as an illegitimate child in his *Maṇimañjarī* (Doniger 1988: 208–209; Granoff 1984: 296). Likewise, the acceptance of Ṛṣabhanātha as an *avatāra* of Viṣṇu was an effort at Vaiṣṇavizing a Jain deity and an ingenious, albeit unsuccessful, "drive towards the syncretism of the two rival faiths" (Jaini 2000: 343–44). Further, the Vedāntist philosopher Mādhava Ācārya (fourteenth century) is often said to have displayed an exemplary tolerance of opposing points of view in his *Śarvadarśanasaṃgraha* (Collection of All Systems), which begins by presenting the school of Cārvākas, criticizes it and ends with Śaṅkara's *Advaita* "as the conclusion and crown of all philosophical systems" (Grimes 2005: 539). What, however, is missed is that this was in keeping with the traditional Indian practice of presenting the opponent's view before refuting it. Similar examples are available from subsequent periods as well. The Muslim sect of Imam Shahis believed that the Imam was himself the tenth *avatāra* of Viṣṇu and that the Qurān was a part of the *Atharvaveda* (Ivanow 1936: 19–70). Christ was sometimes included in the incarnations of Viṣṇu (Danielou 1964: 12) just as Queen Victoria was accepted as a Hindu goddess when a plague broke out in Mumbai following an insult to her statue by some miscreants (Hopkins 1913: 314). What is, however, omitted in all this, is that neither the Imam, nor Christ, nor Victoria occupied an important place in the Brāhmaṇical scheme of things.

II

Even if we accept these instances as evidence of Brāhmaṇism giving space to heterodoxies, there are valid reasons and much historical data to question the view that India has been a land of religious tolerance and that the large number of sects covered by the umbrella term "Hinduism" have stood for nonviolence. Apart from the fact that a religion with a caste system and untouchability as characteristic features was and is inherently incapable of promoting tolerance, sources indicate antagonism between the various Brāhmaṇical sects as well as between Brāhmaṇism, which accepted the Vedic authority, and the heterodox non-Brāhmaṇical sects, which rejected it. Thus the legend of Dakṣa, which evolved from the *Ṛgveda* through Brāhmaṇa literature to the *Mahābhārata* and further to the Purāṇas, which belong to early mediaeval and subsequent times, has been interpreted by scholars as a saga of conflict between Vaiṣṇavism and Śaivism (Doniger 1975: 118; Bhattacharji 2000: 124). It has also been construed as evidence of the struggle between the two cults over a holy place called Kanakhala (near Haridwar), which is highly spoken of in the *Mahābhārata*, and access through which to the river Ganga during the Kumbhamela was given much importance by their adherents.

The Purāṇic and other early Indian texts are, in fact, quite unambiguous about the Śaiva–Vaiṣṇava antagonism. The *Viṣṇupurāṇa* claims the superiority of Viṣṇu over Brahmā and Śiva (*Viṣṇupurāṇa*, I.9.56), and the *Kūrmapurāṇa* considers the various Śaiva sects—Bhairavas, Kāpālikas, Vāmas—as deserving to be censured for deluding the world (Gonda 1976: 92–93). Similarly, the *Varāhapurāṇa* devotes two chapters to the negative portrayal of the Śaiva sect of the Pāśupatas (Gonda 1976: 92–3, 196 n. 55), and the *Padmapurāṇa* (6.234.27) makes the general statement that even a brāhmaṇ is a *pāṣaṇḍa* (hypocrite, impostor) if he is not a Vaiṣṇava (*avaiṣṇas tu yo vipraḥ sa pāṣaṇḍaḥ prakīrtitaḥ*)—an exclusivist position also supported by the *Vṛddhahārita*, a mediaeval legal text, according to which a Vaiṣṇava reciting a *mantra* received from a non-Vaiṣṇava guru will be cooked in the fire of hell for millions of years (Gonda 1976: 93). The *Śaṅkaradigvijaya* recalls a meeting between Mādhava and Śaṅkara, accompanied respectively by the king Sudhanvan and the Kāpālikas. The Kāpālika preceptor reproached the philosopher Mādhava for not worshipping Bhairava, leading to a fight between king Sudhanvan and the Kāpālikas, who were all killed (Gonda 1976: 196–97). Some early mediaeval legal authorities even prescribed purificatory rites for those touching a Śaiva or entering a Śaiva or Buddhist temple (Gonda 1976: 92–93; Kane 1974: II, 1, 168–89). The Vaiṣṇava aversion to the Śaivas is evident from the practice that a "good" Vaiṣṇava would not use even the common word "to sew" (*siv*) because it resembled the name of Śiva—a practice which prevailed among Vaiṣṇavite families until recently (Gonda 1976: 196 n. 58).

The Śaivas seem to have reciprocated the Vaiṣṇava contempt in full measure. They regarded Viṣṇu sometimes as a sorcerer (Meinhard 1928: 38 in Gonda 1976: 196); and the *Saurapurāṇa* (3.6) seeks to prove the superiority of Śiva, who gave the *sudarśanacakra* to Viṣṇu. The *Padmapurāṇa*, which extols the worship of Vāsudeva at one place but discourages it strongly at another, states that let not the name of Viṣṇu ever be pronounced (Rocher 1986: 22). The followers of Śaṅkara "opposed and persecuted" the Vaiṣṇava philosopher Madhu/Madhva (Doniger 1988: 209), and in two chapters the *Saurapurāṇa* bitterly attacks him and describes him "as a cārvāka, a most malignant, disguised promulgator of the defamation of Śiva" and his followers as "wicked creatures...mlecchas, śūdras" (Rocher 1986: 22).

Important evidence of Śaiva intolerance and fanaticism is found in the attitude of the Coḷa ruler Kulottunga II, who removed the statue of Viṣṇu from the courtyard of the Chidambaram temple (Nilakanta Sastri 1975: 644–45), and also in the story of the twenty Śaiva priests committing suicide to protest the introduction of Vaiṣṇavite symbols in it (Gonda 1976: 196 n. 57). This fits in with the story of the persecution of Rāmānuja (1017–1137), who, according to the conventional account, was forced to withdraw from his centre of activity in Srirangam (Tamilnadu) in 1098 to Mysore (Karnataka) for nearly twenty-five years (Nilakanta Sastri 1975: 644; idem 1987: 437); and there is the story of the bigoted Coḷa king who ordered the eyes of one of his disciples to be put out (Gonda 1976: 196 n. 49).

The spiteful attitude of the Śaivas towards the Vaiṣṇavas is evident from an epigraph of 1160, which records the decision of the *mahāsabhā* of Tirukkadaiyūr that the property of a Śaiva who engaged in social intercourse with the other group would be forfeited and made over to the local temple (Nilakanta Sastri 1975: 645). So great was the enmity that a Vaiṣṇava Nāgā, according to one tradition, took a vow not to eat his meal without killing at least one Śaiva monk, and a Śaiva in turn swore never to take his food unless he had slain one Vaiṣṇava (Klostermaier 1990: 335; Ghurye 1964: 177). According to another tradition, two Gosāin leaders had taken a vow to slay two Vairāgīs daily before tasting food (Orr 1940: 86). The most unambiguous example of religious intolerance is, however, provided by the Vīraśaiva hagiographical text which tells us how a Vedāntist was humiliated by Basava at the court of Bijjala and how a Vedic scholar was ridiculed by the Liṅgāyats, who had the Vedas recited by dogs (Nandi 2000: 485 n. 47).

The Śaiva–Vaiṣṇava hostility was not confined to the upper echelons of society. It was seen among lower social ranks as well. An eighteenth-century Tamil work, for example, describes how in their quarrel the Śaiva and Vaiṣṇava wives of a low-caste man dragged their gods in a most unseemly manner (Jesudasan 1961: 246; Gonda 1976: 94). Similarly, in the nineteenth century J. A. Dubois, the French cleric who spent nearly thirty years in India, refers to "numerous troops of religious mendicants and vagabonds always ready to provoke each other and to hurl gross and obscene abuse at each other's heads" (Gonda 1976: 94). One may not be far from the truth in suggesting that these "mendicants and vagabonds" included members of higher as well as lower castes and that different social segments were involved in the Śaiva–Vaiṣṇava conflicts.

III

While instances of the Śaiva–Vaiṣṇava hostility in the early mediaeval and subsequent centuries can be multiplied to almost any length, early Indian sources provide plentiful evidence of conflict between Brāhmaṇism and heterodox sects. An early testimony of the Brāhmaṇical antagonism towards Jainism, for example, comes from its canonical text, *Āyārāṅgasuttam* (XXII, II.3.1.10) according to which monks hid themselves in the day and travelled by night lest they be suspected of being spies. Similarly, the *Arthaśāstra* of Kauṭilya (II.4.23; III.20.16) contemptuously describes the followers of non-Vedic sects as *vṛṣala* or *pāṣaṇḍa*(?) (e.g., Śākyas, Ājīvikas), assigns them residence at the end of or near the cremation ground (*pāṣaṇḍacaṇḍālānām śmasānānte vāsaḥ*), and prescribes a heavy fine for inviting them to dinners in honour of the gods and the manes.

The word *pāṣaṇḍa* in the edict of Aśoka "is not necessarily pejorative," because he appointed *dharmamahāmātras* to look after the affairs of not only the Buddhist Sangha, the brāhmaṇs and Ājīvikas but also "some other religious sects" (*pāṣaṇḍesu*). The toleration of dissenting faiths which was the hallmark of Aśoka's policy is not seen, however, in subsequent times. The celebrated grammarian Patañjali (second century BCE) observed that "the Śramaṇas and Brāhmaṇas are eternal enemies" (*virodhaḥ śāśvatikaḥ*) like the "snake and the mongoose" (*Vyākaraṇa Mahābhaṣya*, 2.4.9; Jaini 2000: 337). The third–fourth century Buddhist work *Divyāvadāna* (1886: 433–44) describes Puṣyamitra Śuṅga as a great persecutor of Buddhists who not only destroyed their *stūpas* but also announced a prize of one hundred *dīnār* for every head of a Śramaṇa.

The Brāhmaṇical animosity towards Buddhism and Jainism seems to have intensified in the early mediaeval period, as is evident from the textual evidence of theological antagonism as well as of the persecution of their adherents. Uddyotakara (seventh century) refuted the Buddhist logicians Nāgārjuna and Dignāg, and his arguments were further reinforced by Vācaspati Miśra (ninth century) who asserted that the Buddhist and Jain doctrines are contradicted by the valid means of knowledge and that the Buddha and Ṛṣabha intended to delude the world—a view repeated by another anti-Buddhist logician Udayana (Granoff 1991–92: 283–84). The founder of the Navya Nyāya school, he launched a sharp attack on the atheistic thesis of Buddhism in his *Ātmatattvaviveka*, a text also known as the *Bauddhadhikāragrantham* on account of its outright rejection of the ideas of Buddhists. He also demolished the ideas of the Saugatas, Digambaras, Cārvākas, Mimāṃsakas and Sāṃkhyas in his *Kusumān-*

jaliprakaraṇa, which he wrote as a commentary on his own work *Nyāyakusumānjali* (Thakur 1964: 72).

Outside the school of Nyāya, several Brāhmaṇical thinkers attacked Buddhism and Jainism. For example, Kumārila Bhaṭṭa (eighth century), the south Indian dialectician, rejected the views of all unorthodox religious movements, especially Buddhism and Jainism, because, according to him, whatever is contradicted by a Vedic statement has to be rejected. He goes to the extent of saying that "they are like ungrateful and alienated children who refuse to acknowledge what they owe to their parents" because they "use the [Vedic] idea of *ahiṃsā* as an instrument of their anti-Vedic propaganda." Śaṅkara, Kumārila's younger contemporary, is even more rigid and uncompromising. He categorically rejects all traditions outside the Vedas, including those of the Bhāgavatas or Pañcarātrins, and accuses the Buddha of "incoherent prattling (*asambaddhapralāpitvāpitvā*) or even deliberately and hatefully leading mankind into confusion..." (Halbfass 1991: 57, 59, 61, 95–6) and Buddhism of an overall inconsistency (*sarvathānupapatti*) (Klostermaier 1979: 69). Similarly, while an inscription dated 1035 (*EI* V [1898–99]: 227) describes a Śaiva temple priest (Lakuliśapaṇḍita? by name) as "a submarine fire in the ocean of Buddhists" (*bauddhābdhi baḍavāmukham*), Madhusūdana Sarasvatī, the sixteenth-century Bengali commentator of the *Bhagavadgītā*, tells us that the teachings of the materialists and the Buddhists *et al.* are like those of the *mlechhas* and excludes them from his consideration (Halbfass 1990: 361).

The attitude of the orthodox philosophers found an echo in the Purāṇic texts as well. According to the *Devīpurāṇa*, Buddhists were a symbol of evil the sight of whom could result in disaster; and their appearance even in dreams was inauspicious (Chakrabarti 2001: 149). Similarly the *Nāradīyapurāṇa* asserts that "a brāhmaṇa who enters a Buddhist temple even in a time of great calamity cannot get rid of the sin by means of hundreds of expiations" (*Nāradīyapurāṇa* I.15.50-2 in Holt 2004: 10). This denigration of dissenting faiths was also extended to Jains, Kāpālikas and Cārvākas, as is indicated by a passage of the *Devībhāgavatapurāṇa* (Chakrabarti 2001: 163 n. 1620). The *Saurapurāṇa* (64.44; 38.54) says that the Buddhists, Jains and Cārvākas should not be allowed to settle in a kingdom.[2]

Similarly, early mediaeval literary texts provide highly negative portrayals of these groups. The *Mattavilāsa Prahasana*, a farce written by the Pallava ruler Mahendravarman (seventh century), depicts Buddhists as morally depraved, dishonest and the scum of the earth. A corrupt Buddhist monk is made to ask, "why did [the Buddha] not think of sanctioning the possession of women and the drinking of *surā* (*kinnukhalu strīparigrahaḥ surāpānavidhānam ca na dṛṣṭam*)?" (1973: 48).

The *Prabodhacandrodaya*, a drama written by Kṛṣṇa Miśra (eleventh century), describes both Buddhism and Jainism as *tāmasika* (arising out of darkness), depicts a Buddhist monk as indulging in worldly pleasures (1998: 70; Act III, verse 9) and a Jain monk as naked, devoid of manliness (*nivīrya*), the hair of his head plucked out and carrying a peacock feather in his hand (1998: 44–45); it also speaks of a battle between good and evil in which Buddhists, Jains, *pāṣaṇḍas* (heretics) and materialists (*Lokāyatas*) were defeated and all the anti-Vedic schools "were uprooted by the sea of the Vedic thoughts" (1998: 126).

The heterodox sects did not lag behind in their denunciation of Brāhmaṇical literature and thought. The Jain logician Akalaṅka (seventh–eighth centuries) was full of scorn for Vedic animal sacrifice, and the famous scholar Hemacandra (twelfth century) dubbed Manu's verses supporting ritual violence as part of *hiṃsāśāstra*. In the seventh century the Jain commentator Jinadāsa described Maheśvara (Śiva) as "the son of a nun who had been magically impregnated by a wizard seeking a suitable repository for his powers" (Dundas 1992: 201); and in the sixteenth century the *Pāṇḍavapurāṇas*, which are the Jainized version of the *Mahābhārata*, show Viṣṇu in a negative light and portray Kṛṣṇa as "scheming and selfish" (Jaini 2000: 353; cf. Dundas 1992: 200–206). While the Jain sources are replete with hostile statements about the Brāhmaṇical sects, they frequently refer to great Jain teachers defeating Buddhists in debate (Dundas 1992: 206–208), and the famous Jain philosopher Haribhadra (eighth century), indeed, critiques Buddhism and Vedānta. The hostility of the Jains towards the Buddhists is also borne out by their appropriation of the caves of the latter (Bhattacharya 1998: 204).

Similarly, the Buddhist contempt for Brāhmaṇism was never a secret. As is well known, the Buddha himself described the three Vedas as a "foolish talk" and "a waterless desert," and their wisdom as "a pathless jungle" and "a perdition" (*Dīghanikāya* I, Tevijjasutta). In early mediaeval times, the Buddhist hostility towards Brāhmaṇism and other religions like Jainism became severe. At the theoretical level this is evident from works like the *Tattvasṃgraha* of Śāntarakṣita (eighth century) who critically reviewed Nyāya, Mimāṃsā, Śāṅkhya and Jain philosophies from the Buddhist point of view.[3] The theological antagonism to Brāhmaṇism also manifested itself in the disdainful attitude of the Buddhists towards Brāhmaṇical deities. They treated several deities, especially the Śaiva ones, as menials and as subordinate to the Buddhist gods and goddesses. They are thus often portrayed in some early mediaeval sculptures as being trampled upon (Sharma 1970: 665–66). Evidence of Buddhist and Jain antipathy towards Śaivism, however, appears to be less voluminous in comparison to the copious references to the Śaiva hostility towards the heterodox sects. So fierce was the opposition of the Śaivites to the heterodox sects that they possibly went to the extent of destroying Buddhist and Jain literary works. There is much substance in the view that religious fanaticism explains the disappearance of important Buddhist works like the *Kuṇṭalakeci* and the *Vimpicārakatai* and of Jain works like the *Vaḷaiyāpati* and the *Rāmāyaṇa*, and even the wilful destruction of the Tamil Siddha works by the orthodox Śaivas (Zvelebil 1992: 46–7).

The Brāhmaṇical *odium theologicum* and the invective against Buddhists and Jains were not empty words; for their persecution from around the middle of the first millennium is amply borne out by early mediaeval sources. Hsüan Tsang states that the Gauḍa king Śaśānka, a contemporary of Harṣavardhana, cut the Bodhi tree at Gaya and removed the statue of the Buddha from the local temple. He also tells us that the Huṇa ruler Mihirakula, a devotee of Śiva, destroyed 1,600 Buddhist stūpas and monasteries and killed thousands of Buddhist monks and laity (Beal 1969: 171–72), his cruelties receiving corroboration from Kalhaṇa (eleventh century), who makes a reference to the persecution of Buddhists by a Kashmir king in the earlier period. Although references to the plunder and destruction of temples found in the *Rājataraṅgiṇī* of Kalhaṇa relate generally to the royal greed for wealth, some of them are certainly indicative of hostility towards the Buddhists. An early example of this is the destruction of a Buddhist *vihāra* by Aśoka's son Jalauka, who was a Śaivite (I.140–44).

Important evidence of the persecution of Buddhists in Kashmir belongs to the reign of king Kṣemagupta (950–58), who destroyed the Buddhist monastery Jayendravihāra at Srinagara and used its ruins in constructing a temple called Kṣemagaurīśvara (*Rājataraṅgiṇī* VI.171-73). In present-day Uttar Pradesh forty-seven deserted sites of fortified towns in Sultanpur district, we are told, are ruins of Buddhist cities destroyed by fire when Brāhmaṇism won its final victory over Buddhism (Yadava 1973: 346). Some Purāṇic passages and inscriptions from northern India also provide evidence of the persecution of the Buddhists. A Tibetan tradition has it that the Kalacuri king Karṇa (eleventh century) destroyed many Buddhist temples and monasteries in Magadha, and the Tibetan text *Pag-sam-jon-zang* refers to the burning of the library of Nalanda by some "Hindu fanatics" (1973: 346), not by Bakhtiyār Khaljī as is commonly believed. An interesting example of antagonism to Buddhists comes from south India. The Vaiṣṇava poet-saint Tirumaṅkai, according to a thirteenth-century Ālvār text, stole a large gold image of the Buddha from a *stūpa* at Nagapattinam and had it melted down for reuse in the temple which he was commissioned by the god Viṣṇu himself to build (Davis 1999: 83). The mediaeval Brāhmaṇical hostility towards and contempt for the Buddhists seem to have continued to our own times in many sections of our society as is evident from the use of the expression *lanja dibbalu* in Telegu, meaning "prostitute hill," for the mounds containing Buddhist archaeological remains (Holt 2004: 10).

IV

While all this points to hostility towards Buddhists, there is much more evidence of antipathy towards and persecution of Jains, especially from south India, where proponents of devotional Śaivism (Nāyanārs) and Vaiṣṇavism (Ālvārs) consistently portrayed them as hated "others" from the sixth–seventh centuries onwards. Evidence of this is available from the *Tevāram* (tenth century), a collection of hymns attributed to the three early and prominent Nāyanār saint-poets. Two of them, Appar (seventh century) and Sambandar (seventh century), denigrated the Jains in abusive language. Appar speaks of them as the "shameless Jain monks," "naked Jains who fast by night," "wicked monks who eat in barbaric ways," "the weak and filthy Jains with their yellowing teeth." Sambandar's denunciation of the Jains is in no better language. He refers to them as "mad Jain monks who wear mats, and pluck their hair and eat their food standing" (Peterson 1998: 171). A vivid description of the encounter of these two Nāyanār saints with Jains is available from the twelfth-century hagiographical work, the *Periyapurāṇam* of Śekkiḷār. The most important and well-known event mentioned in his narrative relates to how Sambandar defeated the Jains in all contests and succeeded in converting the Pāṇḍyan king of Madurai from Jainism to Śaivism, eventually leading to the impalement of eight thousand Jain monks.

Although there is no record of a massacre having taken place (Dundas 1992: 109–19; Davis 1998b: 213–24), the Śaiva intolerance towards the Jains is corroborated by several legends narrated in the *sthalapurāṇa* of Madura (Desai 1957: 82). Similarly, the conversion of the earliest known Jain cave temple in Tirunelveli district (Tamilnadu) into a Śaiva shrine in the seventh century (Thapar 1987: 18; cf. Champakalakshmi 1978: 69–81), the portrayal of the scenes on the walls of the Kailashnath temple of Kanchipuram (Nandi 1986: 97) and those of the *maṇḍapam* of the Golden Lily tank of the Minaksi temple at Madura bear testimony to the persecution suffered by the Jains in Tamilnadu.

In Karnataka, the Jains were a perpetual *bête noire* to the militant Śaivite Liṅgāyat sect which started in the twelfth century. The hagiographies of its leader Bāsava furnish evidence of the slaughter of Jains

(Rao 1990: 200–13), and the conversion of Jain temples at several places in Karnataka into Śaiva shrines and the vandalizing of Jain images are well documented (Thapar 1987: 18). A notable episode of the desecration of a Jain religious establishment, recorded in a Karnataka inscription as well as the *Cennabasava Purāṇa*, took place in 1160 at Ablur when the Vīraśaiva Ekāntada Rāmayya defeated the Jains in debate, demolished their temple and built a shrine in honour of Vīra Somanātha which contains sculptured panels depicting scenes of his encounter with the Jains (*EI*, V [1898–99]: no. 25, lines 69-80; Desai 1957: 182; Lorenzen 1978: 64–5). Their victimization became so severe that the Jains had to seek the intervention of the Vijayanagara ruling family in the fourteenth century. But the Vīraśaivas continued to persecute them in subsequent times. This is borne out by several sixteenth-century inscriptions from the Srisailam area of Andhra Pradesh, one of which tells us that a chief named Liṅga took pride in cutting off the heads of Śvetāmbara Jains (Desai 1957: 23). The Jains remained a hated lot until very much later, and, not surprisingly, a passage of unknown source (Chanana 1965: 65) tells us that one should not enter a Jain temple even under threat of being trampled upon by an elephant (*hastinā taḍyamāno pi na gacched jainamandiram*).

V

Evidently, then, there is considerable evidence to show that the Brāhmaṇical sects did not routinely practise religious tolerance. On the contrary, the increasingly frequent portrayal of brāhmaṇs as engaged in soldierly activities and as receiving military training implies their emergence as a militant group. References to arms-bearing brāhmaṇs are found in several early Indian texts. Pāṇini (c. 500 BC) uses the word "Brāhmaṇaka" for the country in which brāhmaṇs adopted the military profession (IV.2.104), Kauṭilya (IX.2) refers to the recruitment of brāhmaṇ soldiers, and Patañjali (200 BC) speaks of a Śiva Bhāgavata carrying an iron lance (V.2.76).

Such references as these are plentiful in the early mediaeval period. Bāṇabhaṭṭa (seventh century), for example, describes the meeting of Puṣpabhūti with the ascetic Bhairavācārya and three disciples who were valiant fighters and how two of them became personal bodyguards of the king (Agrawal 1964: 56–60). Inscriptions testify to the fact that the early mediaeval ruling houses like the Candellas, Kalacuris, Cālukyas and Rāṣṭrakūṭas quite often employed brāhmaṇ military officers (*EI* IV [1896–97]: 158; *IA* XXV [1896]: 205; *IHQ* IV [1928]: 35). According to a record of 888 CE, a brāhmaṇ called Gaṇaramma laid down his life while defending his village during the reign of Kṛṣṇa III of the Rāṣṭrakūṭa dynasty (*EI* XIII [1915–16]: no.15(i), line 4), which enlisted the service of several brāhmaṇ generals (*EI* XIII [1915–16]: no. 29, lines 9-13). The Coḷa rulers conferred the title *brahmādhirāja* on those brāhmaṇs who distinguished themselves in battle (Mahalingam 1954: 263; Nilakanta Sastri 1975: 456, 465). Brāhmaṇs continued to occupy important military positions in the subsequent period; Kopaṇṇa, a brāhmaṇ general, is said to have been instrumental in extending Vijayanagara power in the Tamil countryside (Shulman 1985: 111). Rummaging through the sources, one gets the impression that the number of arms bearing brāhmaṇs increased in the early mediaeval period and that they came to enjoy much respect in society—which is in keeping with the disdain for temple priests often seen in the early mediaeval normative as well as narrative texts (Chattopadhyaya 1966: 58). Not surprisingly, it was during this period that the concept of *kṣatra-brāhmaṇa* received much attention from jurists.

The frequent mention of arms-bearing brāhmaṇs is indicative of martial skills which they seem to have acquired through military education—a fact amply supported by the early mediaeval epigraphic evidence. According to an analysis of the inscriptional data the term *caṭṭa*, which occurs in inscriptions along with the word *bhaṭṭa*, stands for the brāhmaṇs who received training in martial arts. The word *caṭṭa* found in a record from Parthivapuram (866 CE) has been interpreted to mean brāhmaṇ students who were required not only to study the Vedic lore but also to receive military training in the centres called *śālai* attached to local Viṣṇu temples (Veluthat 1978: 102–15). Several similar temple supported establishments existed in Kerala during the early mediaeval period, an important one being the Kāntalūrśālai, which became famous for its military role in the Coḷa–Cera conflict (Narayanan 1970: 125–36).

The counterparts of *śālais* were called *ghaṭikās* in the Cālukya and Pallava territories, the most famous being the one at Kanchi. That the *śālais* and *ghaṭikās* imparted military education to brāhmaṇs is borne out by literary texts from both north and south India. The Jain work *Kuvalayamālā* of Udyotanasūri (eighth century) describes a *maṭha* at Vijaya where students from different parts of India such as Lāṭa, Karnāṭaka, Mālava, Kannauj, Mahārāṣṭra, Saurāṣṭra, Śrīkaṇṭha and Sindha, received instruction in such diverse subjects as archery (*dhanurveda*), manoeuvring with a shield (*phalakakrīḍā*), use of the sword and the bow (*asi dhanu praveśa*), fighting with a spear (*kuntayuddha*), fighting with clubs (*lakuṭiyuddha*), fighting with arms (*bāhuyuddha*), and so on (Sharma 1996: 231). Similarly, several *maṇipravāla* texts, especially the *Candrotsavam* (fifteenth century) and the *Keralotpatti* (seventeenth century), indicate the association of brāhmaṇs with martial arts. Somadeva (eleventh century) in his *Kathāsaritasāgara* (1960: LXXIV, 155; LXXIII, 69; LVI, 9) makes several references to brāhmaṇs receiving military training. Thus Śrīdarśana, Mahīpāla and Akṣakṣapaṇaka are said to have acquired training in the use of weapons (Chattopadhyaya 1966: 52–59); and some celebrated heroes who figure in this work (e.g., Guṇaśarmaṇa, Aśokadatta, Śaktidatta and Śrīdatta) as experts in the art of warfare also find mention in Kṣemendra's *Bṛhatkthāmañjarī* (Chattopadhyaya 1966: 52). Similar evidence is available from the *Rājataraṅgiṇī* (VII.675; VIII.1071, 1345, 3018) of Kalhaṇa (twelfth century) who refers to several brave brāhmaṇ soldiers who died in battle as well as from inscriptions which speak of the preceptors promoting the study of religious texts from their *maṭhas* having "fortress like structures" and of the pontiffs who are eulogized for their political wisdom, bravery and knowledge of religious texts and weaponry (*śāstra-śastra viśāradaḥ* [*CII* IV, pt. 1, no. 64, verses 23, 44]). The practice of imparting military training to brāhmaṇs led to the emergence of groups of them taking to arms for their livelihood. This perhaps facilitated the establishment of new kingdoms by the armed brāhmaṇ families like the Parivrājakas and also the growth of militias necessary for the protection of the temple wealth—a fact which explains why we get references to fighting ascetics in some early mediaeval texts. The *Bṛhatkathāślokasaṃgraha* of Buddhasvāmin (eighth century), for example, refers to the fighting Pāśupata ascetics who were armed by a guild for the protection of its trading activities (Davidson 2002: 80; Clark 2006: 228), and the *Rājataraṅgiṇī* (VII.1092-1094) tells us that king Harṣa of Kashmir employed naked ascetics (described as "naked wanderers" and "crippled naked wanderers") who raided the temples and defiled the images with spittle and excrement (Basham 1951: 206).

The imparting of martial training to brāhmaṇs also paved the way for the emergence of the military ascetic orders of the Śaṅkara school, known as *Daśanāmī Nāgās* and organized around what are known as *akhāḍās* (Ghurye 1964: chapter IV; Clark 2006: 228–32). Col. James Tod confirms the existence of numerous naked militant ascetics called *nāgās* throughout Rajputana before the thirteenth century, and J. N. Farquhar, who was one of the first to study militant asceticism, speaks of their presence throughout north India from at least the seventh century (Farquhar 1925a: 479–86; 1925b: 431–52; Orr 1940: 81–100; Gross 1992: chapter 2). Similarly Jadunath Sarkar (1958: 82–90; Lorenzen 1978: 69), on the basis of a nineteenth-century Hindi manuscript, dates the establishment of the six armed bands or *akhāḍās* of the Daśanāmī Nāgās between 547 and 1146 CE. While the precise date of the establishment of the *akhāḍās* of the militant Daśanāmī Nāgās appears to be uncertain and calls for a separate study, there is little doubt that they emerged as an important socio-religious factor in the early mediaeval period. Their counterparts, the militant Vaiṣṇava Nāgās, may have organized themselves around *akhāḍās* somewhat later.

In any case, contrary to the view of some scholars (Lorenzen 1978; Pinch 1996), the growth of militant ascetic orders indicates the existence of warrior ascetics and soldier sadhus in India before the coming of Islam and their formation as *akhāḍās* was therefore not in response to their harassment by the Muslims (Clark 2006: 230). They spawned antagonism and armed hostilities between the numerous Brāhmaṇical and non-Brāhmaṇical religions as well as among the various Brāhmaṇical sects in the early mediaeval and subsequent periods, when several instances of armed conflict between the Śaivas and Vaiṣṇavas are recorded. Jadunath Sarkar, on the basis of a traditional account, tells us that the Nāgā Sanyāsis—Bhavānanda, Surasurānanda and Kamalānanda—inflicted a crushing defeat on the Vaiṣṇava Vairāgīs at Haridwar in 1266 and gained precedence in taking bath at the Kumbhamela (Ghurye 1964: 103). The Śaiva and Vaiṣṇava Nāgās again fought at the same place in 1760, and this finally settled the issue of bathing precedence in favour of the former (Klostermaier 1991: 112).

There is also the evidence to indicate that a large number of Vairāgīs were massacred at the Simhasta fair at Nasik in 1690 (Ghurye 1964: 178) and that an open confrontation between the Śaiva Sanyāsis and Vaiṣṇava Vairāgīs took place at Ayodhya after the death of Aurangzeb over control of religious places and pilgrims' fees and gifts (Sharma 2000: 14-15; Bakker 1986: 149). In fact regular battles between the Daśanāmīs and Vaiṣṇava Vairāgīs seem to have taken place until as late as the nineteenth century. All this suggests that, like mediaeval Christianity and Islam, Brāhmaṇism and its various sects were inherently intolerant and that their intolerance, often expressed through violence, may have received much sustenance from the martialization of the religious sects in the early mediaeval period. It is thus difficult to agree with the view that "Hinduism" has "a propensity to assimilate rather than to exclude" or that tolerance is the very essence of "Hinduism qua Hinduism" (Sharma 1978: 145). Equally, to say that Islam brought violence to a land which until its arrival had lived in religious harmony is to blind oneself to a *mélange* of available evidence.

VI

It is evident from the above discussion that several Brāhmaṇical and heterodox religious sects existed in India in the early mediaeval period before the coming of Islam. In this atmosphere of religious pluralism marked by several competing soteriological perspectives, the Brāhmaṇical religious preceptors often tried to convert people to their own sects. Since the Brāhmaṇical sects—covered by the modern term "Hinduism"—did not have a founder, a basic text or an organized monastic establishment, they may not have proselytized in the same manner as Christianity or Islam. But sources indicate that Brāhmaṇical conversion was practised in early India before as well as after the advent of Islam. As early as the later Vedic period, the *Tāṇḍya Brāhmaṇa*, also known as the *Pañcaviṃśa Brāhmaṇa*, describes the *vrātyastoma* sacrifice which the *vrātya*s (the people living outside the pale of the Brāhmaṇical religion) were required to perform in order to become eligible to have social intercourse with the orthodox āryas (Kane 1974: II, pt. 1, 385–89; Gonda 1977: 539, 641; Heesterman 1962–63: 2). First mentioned in the *Atharvaveda*, the *vrātya*s continued to figure in many post-Vedic texts. Some mediaeval works like the *Vrātyatāprāyaścitanirṇaya* and the *Vrātyatāśuddhisaṃgraha*, on the basis of ancient texts, provide for the purification of *vrātya*s even after twelve generations, though the latter states categorically that they can be admitted into Brāhmaṇical society only in accordance with the prescribed purificatory methods (Choudhary 1964: 77).

Mention may also be made of the *dīkṣā* ceremony, generally understood in the sense of initiation or consecration, which "implies death to profane existence, enables man to gain sacred knowledge and wisdom, a higher stage of existence and access to heavenly life" (Gonda 1965: 316). Without expatiating on the meaning and significance of this ceremony in the various ritual contexts, it may be pointed out that its importance in different Indian religions can hardly be exaggerated. In Vaiṣṇavism, for example, its main object is purification, without which an individual cannot be admitted to the religious order or community and cannot be allowed to read such texts as the *Rāmāyaṇa* or the *Śrībhāṣya* of Rāmānuja (Gonda 1965: 398, 402). The *Bhāgavatapurāṇa*, a fundamental Vaiṣṇava text, states that "those desirous of *mokṣa* must put themselves under the care and guidance of a preceptor," just as the *Haribhaktivilāsa*, the basic text of the Caitanya movement, asserts that "a man without *dīkṣā* is not entitled to worship, for the act of initiation destroys all sins and bestows divine knowledge" (Gonda 1965: 422, 427). Similarly, in Kashmir Śaivism, *dīkṣā* is "the most important method of attaining integral Śivahood"; and in Vīraśaivism it is mandatory for all members of the Vīraśaiva community because it opens the door of Vīraśaivism not only for them but, more importantly, for every non-Vīraśaiva seeking admission to the fold (Gonda 1965: 433; Sadasivaiah 1967: 104–106).

Thus, at least in some cases, *dīkṣā* may be treated as a precondition of conversion to a faith. Even if there are some differences of opinion about the nature and significance of this ritual (Heesterman 1962–63: 2), the practice of religious conversion in Śaivite sects seems to have been common, as can be inferred from a variety of sources like mythology, religious texts, secular literature, and so on. Among the early myths the legend of Dakṣa Prajāpati implies religious conversion within the fold of Brāhmaṇism. It has many versions but its core element is "the conflict between the Vedic sacrificial religion and the Rudra-Śiva religion—which was reconceived into a conflict between Vaiṣṇavism and Śaivism" in the epics and in the Purāṇic texts, the latter belonging mostly to the early mediaeval and subsequent centuries. The climax of the story is represented by Śiva destroying the sacrifice performed by Dakṣa followed by the latter's realization of the superiority of the former and conversion to him (Klostermaier 1991: 110, 125, 128; Bhattacharji 2000: 124).

Besides, the actual conversion procedure is laid down in some texts. For example, the *Somaśambhūpaddhati*, a manual compiled by Somaśambhū in the second half of the eleventh century (von Stietencron 1995: 51–81) prescribes a procedure called the *liṅgoddhāra* (conversion ritual), for converting from other creeds to Śaivism by the ritual removal of earlier religious affiliation, the purpose of the conversion being the realization that without becoming a Śaiva salvation remains unattainable (Michaels 2005: 20–21). Similarly, a Tāntric text called the *Kubjikānityāhnikatilaka* (1197) mentions the conversion of nine Buddhists to the Kaula religion. According to the tradition recorded in it, when Śrīnātha alias Tūṣṇīśa alias Unmanīśanātha, the first of the ancient gurus of the Kubjikā school of Tantra, went to the land of the gandharvas (*gandharvaloka*), he was questioned by some Buddhists living there. He told them that he was a *siddha* (one who is accomplished) and possessed the supreme divine instruction (*divyajñānavaralabdhaka*), upon which the Buddhists laughed at him and challenged him to prove his statement. Śrīnātha, as the story goes, uttered the syllable HUM and all the Buddhist monasteries collapsed. The monks then acknowledged his authority, and later he converted them (*Ṣaṭsāhasra Saṃhitā* 1982: 38; Goudriaan and Gupta 1981: 149). Among the secular works, the *Prabodhacandrodaya* of Kṛṣṇa Miśra (eleventh century) depicts how, after an interesting conversation with a Buddhist and a Jain, and after offering them wine and women, a Kāpālika succeeds in converting them to Śaivism (Act III).

Several legends indicate that religious conversion may have been of central importance to the many *bhakti* saints and gurus who appeared on the religious scene with the development of the various devotional sects, especially in early mediaeval south India, and who were inspired by a strong missionary zeal to convert the people to a life of spiritual surrender to the highest god. This is corroborated by the instances of conversion recorded in the early mediaeval Śaiva hagiographies. The twelfth-century work *Periyapurāṇam* of Śekkiḷār tells us that the Nāyanār saint Appar was born in an orthodox Śaiva family of the Veḷḷāḷa community but became a Jain monk at an early age. Agitated, his elder sister sought Śiva's help. Appar was then afflicted with a serious abdominal disorder, which was cured not by the Jain physicians and their mantras but only by the grace and miracle of Śiva. Repentant over his earlier conversion to Jainism, he came back to the fold of his family faith. Enraged at this, the Jains brought charges against him before the Pallava king Mahendravarman, who was a follower of Jainism. Appar, however, succeeded in convincing the king of the truth of Śaivism, whereupon Mahendravarman himself became a Śaiva. Although the various assumptions underlying this narrative, related in the *Periya-purāṇam* five centuries after the events, have been rightly questioned (Davis 1998b: 213–24), it is true that Appar and Mahendravarman changed their religions.

Śekkiḷār also gives an account of the encounter between another Śaiva saint, Sambandar, and the Jains. As the story goes, the queen and the minister of the Pāṇḍyan king invited Sambandar to Madurai to drive out the Jain monks who exercised a hold over the king. The saint went to Madurai, proved the superiority of his miracles over those of the Jains, and converted the king to Śaivism. The king later impaled eight thousand Jains (Davis 1998b: 213–24; Dundas 1992: 109–10). Like the story of the conversion of Mahendravarman, that of the Pāṇḍyan ruler's embracing Śaivism may be a tall tale told by Śekkiḷār; but in neither of the two cases can the fact of conversion be questioned.

In addition to miracles, theological disputations also seem to have played a role in the spread of Brāhmaṇical religious and philosophical ideas. Of the many early mediaeval Indian philosophers to whom attention has been drawn previously and who engaged in theological polemics, Śaṅkara (eighth century) was by far the most important. A peripatetic mendicant (*parivrājakācārya*), he travelled from place to place and engaged in debates with various sects like the Jains and the Buddhists and refuted their philosophies. He is also said to have converted some individuals to his Advaita philosophy. For instance, he won arguments with Viśvarūpa in Magadha and Maṇḍana in Prayāga, the two disciples of the Mīmāṃsā philosopher Kumārila (Pandey 1994: 278–81, 342). Śaṅkara is also credited with the setting up of four, five or even six monastic establishments in different parts of the country for the mendicants following his doctrines. Despite the conflicting chronological sequence of their establishment, the Śaṅkarite monasteries, in all probability, played an important role in converting people, especially several centuries later under the Vijaynagara rulers whose generous patronage added economic affluence and feudal authority to their traditional religious prestige and influence (Pandey 1994: 36). Śaṅkara's early disciples founded the Daśanāmī orders, to which they converted mendicants and ascetics. This receives corroboration from the *Nārada-parivrājakopaniṣad*, a mediaeval text which sets out in detail the way in which renouncers were to be converted or admitted to these groups (Ghurye 1964: 93; Chakraborty 1973: 58, 61, 119, 144).

Despite the fact that people could be converted through theological debates and disputations, the use of force in drawing people into Śaivite cults was not unknown. In a story related in the *Māghamāhātmya*, which claims to be part of the *Padmapurāṇa*, the Śaivas instigated the kṣatriya king Citrasena of "Draviḍa viṣaya" to prohibit the worship of Viṣṇu in his kingdom, to persecute his devotees, and to have his images thrown into the ocean. As a result, many of his Vaiṣṇava subjects fled the country and those staying back became Śaivas (Hazra 1963: II, 362). One is also reminded of the legend about the battle between Khaṇḍobā, the principal non-brāhmaṇ god of the Western Deccan, and the two demon brothers Malla and Maṇi preserved in the *Mallārīmāhātmya*, which is part of the *Brahmāṇḍapurāṇa*. In this narrative, all of Malla's generals were defeated until only Maṇi was left. Maṇi too was defeated, and just as the sole of Khaṇḍobā's feet touched the head of this demon, he experienced a total change of heart (Stanley 1990: 271–98; Sontheimer 1997: 208–35).

The most unambiguous evidence of forced conversion, however, comes from Karnataka and relates to the persecution of Jains by Vīraśaivas. According to a tradition supported by epigraphic evidence, large-scale conversions from Jainism to Vīraśaivism took place in Karnataka in the wake of Ekāntada Rāmayya's victory over the Jains (Desai 1957: 182–83), and these could not have been different from forced ones. The Vīraśaivas, in fact, engaged in conversion activities in a systematic manner; for the chief function of the monastery founded by Basava at Kalyana in 1156, as well as that of the five traditional Vīraśaiva monasteries established in the different parts of India after the twelfth century, was to convert people to Vīraśaivism (Sadasivaiah 1967: 88–9). Such testimony as cited above certainly indicates that the Brāhmaṇical sects forced people to convert, and one feels that Islam and Christianity have undeservedly earned the sole credit for forced religious conversions.

While the evidence cited indicates that sometimes people were coerced to convert, there is also much to show that this was not always the case. The Purāṇas, most of which were composed in the early mediaeval and subsequent centuries, played a crucial role in changing the religion of the people in large parts of the country. As noted earlier, they launched bitter attacks on heterodox sects like Buddhism and Jainism, which engaged in proselytizing activities, as can be inferred from a passage of the *Viṣṇupurāṇa* (III.8) which tells us that the Buddha came to the earth in order to brainwash the *daityas* against the Vedas (Nath 2001: 195). The Purāṇas thus provided an ideological resistance to the conversion of people to non-Brāhmaṇical sects and were "anxious to ensure that at least brāhmaṇas did not become Buddhists which, they feared, would happen in the degenerate Kali age" (Chakrabarti 2001: 149). But in resisting the heterodoxies they also acted as an instrument for the diffusion of Brāhmaṇical religious ideas among a variety of ethnic groups living in the peripheral areas (Nath 2001: chapter 8; Chakrabarti 2001: chapter IV). Thus, while the Purāṇas played a dual role, it does not seem to have been accompanied by the use of force.

The importance of the Purāṇas in the religious and cultural transformation of non-Brāhmaṇical people should be seen in conjunction with the evidence from the large number of inscriptions which record gifts of land and other objects to temples and priests. These give the unmistakable impression that the practice of making donations to priests and temples in peripheral areas became widespread in the early mediaeval period. As a result, brāhmaṇ settlements mushroomed in different parts of the country and acquired a special significance in the economically backward regions inhabited by culturally marginalized tribal people. In these areas, the brāhmaṇs, living as they did at a higher level of material existence, were able to disseminate their own worldview, especially religious beliefs and practices rooted in the Purāṇas. The popularization of the Purāṇas and the practice of making land grants in the peripheral areas thus went hand in hand and acted as agents of religious transformation as well as of the integration of a large number of ethnic groups into Brāhmaṇical society. This is clear from the fact that the land charters often specified the donees' obligations, which included not only the teaching of Vedic lore but also, more importantly, the performance of Brāhmaṇical rites and rituals which enabled them to make inroads into tribal society and religion. An interesting eighth-century inscription from the Raipur district in Chhattisgarh (Sastri 1995: 154–59) mentions two Śaiva ascetics, Sadyaḥśivācārya and Sadāśivācārya, and records the dedication of a temple to the latter and his spiritual successors along with several plots of black-soil land (*kṛṣṇatala*) located in different villages. It states that the ascetics, in return for the endowment, were to arrange a free feeding house (*annasya sattram*), a sacrificial rite (*yāga*), the exposition of the Śaiva doctrine (*vyākhyāyaḥsamayasya*) and the ceremony of initiation (*dīkṣā*) into the Śaiva faith which was capable of securing salvation (*nirvāṇadakṣa*). This inscription clearly indicates that land gifts were made to priests in the peripheral areas often with the specific purpose of transmitting religious beliefs and practices to tribal groups and converting them to Brāhmaṇical sects.

The growing hegemony of the brāhmaṇs, who received donations of land and other objects in the economically backward areas, led not only to the drawing of various non-Brāhmaṇical groups into the Brāhmaṇical social and religious order through the dissemination of Purāṇic lore and other Brāhmaṇical ideas but also to the appropriation and Brāhmaṇization of more and more of the tribal cults in different parts of the country during the early mediaeval period. In Bengal, for example, Manasā was integrated into the Brāhmaṇical pantheon in the early phase of the Pāla rule; and in Orissa, Maṇināgeśvarī was elevated to a place of importance in the fifth–sixth centuries through royal donations just as Stambheśvarī, a goddess associated with the Śaulika tribe, was absorbed through the patronage of the Śūlkī rulers. In Tamilnadu the goddess Mīnākṣī (fish-eyed) was brought into the Brāhmaṇical fold through the patronage of the Pāṇḍya rulers and in Andhra Pradesh, the goddess Padmāvatī, who has Tāntric affiliations, became important in the eighth century when a temple was built to her at Tirupati. Almost all the temples of the sixty-four *yoginīs* (the mother goddess in sixty-four forms) were built in the tribal belt of eastern Madhya Pradesh and Orissa during early mediaeval times, not to mention several other tribal deities who were drafted into the Tāntric Brāhmaṇical tradition (Jha 2004: 205). The conversion of tribal peoples and the Brāhmaṇization or Sanskritization of their cult deities has been going on until our own times. Scholars often prefer to describe this as acculturation, but in reality it is no different from conversion. The difference between the two is that the former is a protracted process while the latter involves, at least ideally, an abrupt and total switching of religious loyalties.

Religious conversion, through choice and conviction or through coercion and cajolery, was practised by Brāhmaṇical sects in early India and may have received ideological support from early mediaeval normative texts, some of which give sanction to the conversion of those who voluntarily or under compulsion had given up the religions into which they were born. For example, the *Devalasmṛti* (Kane 1974: II, pt. 1: 389–91) states that if brāhmaṇs and members of other castes are carried off by *mleccha*s and indulge in forbidden acts, they can be purified by the performance of appropriate penance (*prāyaścitta*). Its reconstructed text (Wadekar 1996) devotes one full chapter to *mlecchitaśuddhi* and lays down detailed procedures for the purification of those who were taken away by *mlecchas* or stayed with them for five to twenty years.

According to Devala and other early mediaeval lawgivers, anyone who had left his religion could be reconverted and taken back into its fold. Reconversion (*parāvartana*), equated with the ancient ritual of *Vrātyastoma* (Kane 1974: IV, 118), was no different from conversion. There is nothing to show that the *mlecchas*, as distinct from those who joined their ranks by pollution, were not allowed to convert to the Brāhmaṇical religion, because the word *mleccha* occurring in early Indian sources remained a generic term for exclusion and stood for specific tribes or groups of tribes until as late as the fifteenth century, when it came to be used extensively for Muslims (Thapar 2000: 259). This idea of reconversion certainly anticipated the *śuddhi* movement led by the Arya Samaj in the nineteenth century. It is the same as the religious conversion supported by the Ramakrishna Mission, founded in 1897 by Vivekananda, who "wished to flood the country of the Yankees with idolatrous missionaries" and had "grandiose ideas of how the U.S. and Europe could be converted…in a matter of decades" (Brekke 2002: 48; cf. Hacker 1978: 565–79). Nor, finally, does it differ from what is nowadays being aggressively pushed by the Vishwa Hindu Parishad and the numerous other affiliates of the Rashtriya Sawyamsevak Sangh in India and abroad.

In sum, it may be pointed out that one notices several important trends in the religious life of the people of early India. In the first place, there existed numerous religious sects in different parts of the country. Secondly, religious pluralism led to antagonism not only between the different Brāhmaṇical sects but also between them and the heterodox religions such as Buddhism and Jainism. This resulted in both theological and philosophical antagonisms and in violent clashes. Thirdly, the competing, antagonistic and fanatical soteriologies inspired the religious preceptors to convert people to their faiths. The Brāhmaṇical sects, inherently intolerant as they have been, engaged in converting people during the early mediaeval period as well as in our own times. All this militates against the cliché of Hinduism's so-called inherent tolerance, though it does not deny the fact that religious sects borrowed a great deal from one another, leading to the growth of a composite culture over the centuries. But that is a story I propose to tell elsewhere.

3 Holy Cow: Elusive Identity

I

An average Indian of today, rooted in his (supposedly) traditional Hindu religious heritage, carries the misconception that his ancestors, especially the Vedic Āryans, attached great importance to the cow on account of its inherent "sacredness." The "sacred" cow has come to be considered a symbol of community identity of the Hindus whose cultural tradition is often imagined as threatened by the Muslims who are thought of as beef-eaters. The sanctity of the cow has, therefore, been announced with the flourish of trumpets and has been wrongly traced back to the Vedas, which are supposedly of divine origin and the fountainhead of all knowledge and wisdom. In other words, some sections of Indian society have traced back the concept of 'holy' cow to the very period when it was sacrificed and its flesh was eaten.

Since the Brāhmaṇical injunctions against beef eating led to the veneration of the cow in the mediaeval period, it tended to become a political instrument at the hands of rulers. The Mughal emperors (e.g. Bābar, Akbar, Jahāngīr and Aurangzeb, and so on), thus imposed a restricted ban on cow slaughter to accommodate the Jaina or Brāhmaṇical feeling of respect for the cow (Ram 1927: 122–3, 179–90). Similarly Shivaji, sometimes viewed as an incarnation of God who descended on earth for the deliverance of the cow and brāhmaṇ, is described as proclaiming: "We are Hindus and the rightful lords of the realm. It is not proper for us to witness cow slaughter and the oppression of brāhmaṇas" (Ram 1927: 191). But the cow became a tool of mass political mobilization when the organized Hindu cow protection movement, beginning with the Sikh Kuka (or Namdhari) sect in the Punjab around 1870 and later strengthened by the foundation of the first Gorakshini Sabha in 1882 by Dayanananda Saraswati, made this animal a symbol to unite a wide-ranging people, challenged the Muslim practice of its slaughter and provoked a series of serious communal riots in the 1880s and 1890s. There was undoubtedly a "dramatic intensification" of the cow protection movement when in 1888 the North-Western Provinces High Court decreed that a cow was not a sacred object (Frietag 1996: 217). Not surprisingly cow slaughter very often became the pretext of many Hindu–Muslim riots, especially towards the end of the nineteenth century. The killing of the kine emerged again and again as a troublesome issue on the Indian political scene throughout the twentieth century and has become a rallying point for communalists in India, and even Mohandas Karamchand Gandhi, the apostle of peace and communal harmony, believed that cow protection was the "central fact of Hinduism" (Margul 1968: 64). The veneration of this animal has been converted into a symbol of communal identity of the Hindus and the obscurantist and fundamentalist forces obdurately refuse to appreciate that the "sacred" cow was not always all that sacred in the Vedic and subsequent Brāhmaṇical and non-Brāhmaṇical traditions and that its flesh, along with other varieties of meat, was quite often part of the *haute cuisine* in early India. Although the Shin, Muslims of Dardistan in Pakistan, look on the cow as other Muslims do the pig, avoid direct contact with cows, refuse to drink cow's milk or use cow dung as fuel and reject beef as food (Simoons 1979: 468), the self-styled custodians of non-existent "monolithic" Hinduism assert that the practice of beef eating was first introduced in India by the followers of Islam who came from outside and were foreigners in this country, little realizing that their Vedic ancestors were also foreigners who ate the flesh of the cow and various other animals. Fanaticism getting precedence over fact, it is not surprising that the Rashtriya Svayamsevak Sangh (RSS), the Vishwa Hindu Parishad and their numerous outfits have a national ban on cow slaughter on their agenda. So high-geared has been the propaganda about abstention from beef eating as a characteristic trait of modern-day "Hinduism" that when the RSS tried to claim Sikhs as Hindus, it led to a vehement opposition from them and one of the Sikh youth leaders proposed, "Why not slaughter a cow and serve beef in a gurudwara *langar*?" (Ramachandran, *Hindustan Times*, 7 May 2000).

The response of historical scholarship to the communal perception of Indian food culture, however, has been sober and scholars have drawn attention to the textual evidence of beef eating which, in fact, begins to be available from the oldest Indian religious text *Ṛgveda*, supposedly of divine origin. H. H. Wilson, writing in the first half of the nineteenth century, had asserted that "the sacrifice of the horse or of the cow, the *gomedha* or *ashvamedha*, appears to have been common in the earliest periods of the Hindu ritual"—a view convincingly put forth by Rajendra Lal Mitra whose article on the subject formed a chapter of his book *The Indo-Aryans* published in 1881. In 1894 William Crooke, a British civil servant, collected an impressive amount of ethnographic data on popular Indian religious beliefs and practices in his two-volume work and devoted one whole chapter to the respect shown to animals including the cow (Crooke 1978). Later in 1912, he published an informative piece on the sanctity of the cow in India. But he also drew attention to the old practice of eating beef and its survival in his own times (Crooke 1912: 275–306). In 1927, L. L. Sundara Ram (1927) made a strong case for cow protection for which he sought justification from the scriptures of different religions including Hinduism. However, he did not deny that the Vedic people ate beef, though he blamed the Muslims for cow slaughter. Later in the early forties P. V. Kane in his five-volume monumental work *History of Dharmaśāstra* referred to Vedic and early Dharmaśāstric passages which speak of cow killing and beef eating. Similarly, Laxman Shastri Joshi (1972: 83–87), a Sanskritist of unquestionable scholarship, drew attention to the *Dharmaśāstra* works, which unequivocally support the prevalence of the practice of flesh eating including beef eating in early India, and H. D. Sankalia (1967) reinforced the scholarly view on the basis of both literary and archaeological evidence. While the contribution of the scholars mentioned above cannot be minimized, the limitation of their work lies in the fact that they have referred to isolated bits of information on beef, concentrating mainly on the Vedic texts without treating those as part of a flesh-eating tradition prevalent in India. But there is sufficient Indian textual evidence of cattle killing and beef eating widely dispersed over time so as to indicate its continuity for a long time in the Brāhmaṇical society and to suggest that the idea of cow's supposed sanctity/holiness does not tie up with practices prevalent in Indian society.

II

The early Aryans came to India as a semi-nomadic people with a dominantly pastoral economy, in which cattle rearing played an important role and agriculture occupied a secondary place. They inherited their pastoral economy from their Indo-European past, which showed up prominently in different aspects of their life including their religious beliefs and practices. Like pastoralism, they brought from outside the practice of animal or cattle sacrifice, widely prevalent among the early Aryans. It has been suggested on the basis of linguistic and archaeological evidence that the practice of cattle sacrifice of the Vedic period, called *paśubandha*, can be traced in the chronologically earlier steppe cultures of Eastern Europe (Sharma 1996: 42). Nearer home in ancient Iran through which the eastern branch of Indo-Europeans migrated to India, the *Zend Avesta* (1883–87, SBE XXIII, pt. 2, 62, 63, 79; IV, 232–33) bears ample testimony of animal sacrifice and the Vedic term *yajña* (= sacrifice) occurs as *yasna* in this text. It speaks of the sacrifice of 100 oxen and 1,000 small cattle, in addition to that of 100 horses, 10,000 sheep or goats and 1,000 camels just as the Vedic texts frequently refer to the sacrifice of cattle, horses, sheep, goats and pigs.

The *Ṛgveda* frequently refers to the cooking of the flesh of the ox for offering to gods, especially Indra, the greatest of the Vedic gods. At one place he is stated to have said: "they cook for me 15 plus twenty oxen" (X.86.14ab). At other places he is said to have eaten the flesh of bulls (X.28.3c), of one (X.27.2c) or of a hundred buffaloes (VI.17.11b) or 300 buffaloes roasted by Agni (V.29.7ab) or a thousand buffaloes (VIII.12.8ab). Second in importance to Indra is Agni who has some 200 hymns to himself in the *Ṛgveda* (Keith 1970: 154). Born of the mythic parents, Dyaus and Pṛthivī, the god Agni, unlike the licentious Indra, drank Soma moderately, his main food being *ghee*. Protector of all men, he is, nevertheless, described in the *Ṛgveda* as "one whose food is the ox and the barren cow" (VIII.43.11 in Kane 1974: II, 2, 772 n. 1847). There is indeed nothing in the text to indicate his aversion to the flesh of the cattle and other animals. On the contrary, horses (*aśva*), bulls (*ṛṣabha*), oxen (*ukṣan*, Falk 1982: 176), barren(?) cows (*vaśā*, Srinivasan 1979: 58–60) and rams (*meṣa*) were sacrificed for him (X.19.14ab; Shastri 1988: 101–2). In a passage dealing with the disposal of the dead, clear reference is made "to the burning of a goat which is the share of Agni, and to the use of the flesh of the cow to protect the body against the flame" (X.16.4ab; X.16.7ab; Keith 1970: 419). Third in order of importance was the god Soma whose name is derived from a plant which was the source of a heady drink. It has been suggested that "the fundamental and typical Vedic sacrifices are those of Soma" (Renou 1971: 104) in which the killing of animals including cattle played a crucial role (Keith 1970: 327). There was not much variation in the menu of the Ṛgvedic gods. Milk, butter, barley, oxen, goats and sheep were their usual food, though apparently some of them had their preferences. Indra, for example, had a special liking for bulls and the guardian of the roads, Pūṣan, being devoid of teeth, ate mush as a Hobson's choice (Keith 1970: 87).

The later Vedic texts provide detailed descriptions of sacrifices and frequently refer to ritual cattle slaughter and the *Gopatha Brāhmaṇa* alone mentions twenty-one *yajñas* (Thite 1975: chapter VI) though all of them may not have involved animal killing. A bull (*vṛṣabha*) was sacrificed to Indra, a dappled cow to the Maruts and a copper coloured cow to the Aśvins. A cow was also sacrificed to Mitra and Varuṇa (Sharma 1983: 119). In most of the public sacrifices (e.g. *aśvamedha*, *rājasūya* and the *vājapeya*) flesh of various types of animals, especially that of the cow/ox/bull was required. The *agnyādheya*, which was a preparatory rite preceding all public sacrifices, required a cow to be killed (Renou 1971: 102). In the *aśvamedha* (horse sacrifice), the most important of the Vedic public sacrifices first referred to in the *Ṛgveda*[1] and discussed in the Brāhmaṇas, more than 600 animals (including the wild ones like boars) and birds were killed and its *finale* was marked by the sacrifice of twenty-one sterile cows (Renou 1971: 109). The *gosava* (cow sacrifice) was an important component of the *rājasūya* and *vājapeya* sacrifices (Mitra 1969: I, 361)[2] and in the latter, the *Śatapatha Brāhmaṇa* tells us, a sterile spotted cow was offered to Maruts (Thite 1975: 77). Similarly a sterile cow was sacrificed in the *agniṣṭoma* (Renou 1971: 105; Kane 1974: II, 2, 1158) just as the "immolation" of seventeen "dwarf heifers under three" (Mitra 1969: I, 363)[3] was an important element in the *pañcaśāradīyasava* (*darśapūrṇamāsa*). The killing of animals including cattle (*paśu*)[4] figures in several other *yajñas* including *cāturmāsya* (Keith 1970: 323; Heesterman 1957: 28), *sautrāmaṇi* (Kane 1974: II, pt. 2, 1224; Thite 1975: 83–9),[5] and independent animal sacrifice called *paśubandha* or *niruḍhapaśubandha* (Keith 1970: 324; Kane 1974: II, pt. 2, chapter XXXII), which was also an important component of many sacrifices. The *Taittirīya Brāhmaṇa* (III.9.8.I) unambiguously refers to the sacrificial killing of the cow which "is verily food" (*atho annaṃ vai gauḥ*), and praises Agastya for his sacrifice of a hundred bulls (Achaya 1999: 145). That the flesh of the sacrificial victim was meant for human consumption is clear from passages which discuss the mode of cutting up the immolated animal and the distribution of its flesh by the *samitāṛa* who kills the victim by strangulation.[6] There is thus evidence to show that the flesh of the sacrificed cattle was consumed by various categories of people.

Cattle and other animals were killed not only in public sacrifices but also in ordinary and domestic rites of daily life. The later Vedic and post-Vedic texts mention many rites and rituals associated with agricultural and other activities and, in at least some of them, the killing of animals including cattle was *de rigueur*. Among the rites relating to agriculture, which tended to become stable from the later Vedic period onwards, mention may be made of the *śūlagava* (sacrifice of "the ox on the spit").[7] In this sacrifice a spit-ox was killed for Rudra; its tail and skin etc. were thrown into the fire and its blood was poured out on the *kuśa* or *darbha* grass for the snakes (Keith 1970: 364).

An interesting rite repeatedly mentioned in the texts from the later Vedic period onwards is the one relating to the reception of guests and is called *arghya*, or more popularly, *madhuparka*. The killing of the kine to honour guests seems to have been prevalent from earlier times. The *Ṛgveda* mentions (X.68.3) the word *atithinīr*, which has been interpreted as "cows fit for guests" (Tull 1996: 229)[8] and refers to a Vedic hero, Atithigva, whose name literally means "slaying cows for guests."[9] The cow was also killed on festive occasions like marriage. A Ṛgvedic passage (X.85.13c), for instance, refers to the slaughter of a cow on the occasion of marriage (*aghāsu hanyate gāvo*) and, later, in the *Aitareya Brāhmaṇa*, we are told that "if the ruler of men comes as a guest or any one else deserving of honour comes, people kill a bull or a cow."[10] It was performed in honour of special guests, namely the teacher, the priest, a *snātaka*, father-in-law, paternal and maternal uncles, a friend and a king. Their reception not only included the offering of a mixture of curds and honey (whence the term *madhuparka* was derived) but, more importantly, of a cow which was either immolated[11] or let loose according to their wishes, though in no case was the rite performed without beef or flesh-meat (*ĀśGS*, I.24.33; *KāṭhGS*, 24.20; *ŚāṅkhGS*, II.15.2; *PārGS*, I.3.29). Several Gṛhyasūtras describe *madhuparka* both independently[12] as well as part of the marriage ceremonies in which cow was slain more than once in honour of guests.[13] In subsequent times Pāṇini, therefore, uses the term *goghna* for a guest (*Aṣṭādhyāyī*, 3.4.73; Agrawal 1963: 100).[14]

The Gṛhyasūtras also attest to the use of the hide of the bull or the cow in domestic rituals (*PārGS*, I.8.10)[15] like the *sīmantonnayana* (lit. parting of the hair of the woman upwards) ceremony performed in the fourth month of pregnancy (*ĀśGS*, I.14.3) and the *upanayana*, investiture ceremony preceding the beginning of one's studenthood (*PārGS*, II.5.17-20; Kane 1974: II, pt. 1, 278). Cattle, in fact, seem to have been killed even on a flimsy ground; for an Upaniṣadic passage recommends that if one were eager to beget a learned son with a long life he could eat a mess of veal or beef or of other flesh with rice and ghee (*Bṛ. Up.*, VI.4.18),[16] though six months after the birth the child itself could be fed on the flesh of birds (e.g., *bhāradvājī*, *tittira*, *kṛkasā*, etc.) and fish (Gopal 1959: 278).

The practice of cattle killing was also intimately connected with the cult of the dead, which occupies considerable space in the Vedic as well as post-Vedic texts. One (X.16.7ab) of the several Ṛgvedic passages (X.14-18) relating to cremation, for example, refers to the use of the skin and the thick fat of the cow to cover the dead body, and the *Atharvaveda* at one place speaks of a bull "presumably being burnt along with the dead to ride with in the next world."[17] The Gṛhyasūtras, elaborately describing the funerary procedure, provide ample evidence of cattle killing at the time of cremation and of the practice of distributing different limbs of the animal on those of the corpse.[18] The cremation was followed by several rites performed in honour of the Manes, variously mentioned as *pitṛryajña*, *mahāpitṛyajña* and *aṣṭakā* in the Vedic passages and as some other types of *śrāddha* discussed in the post-Vedic texts, especially the Gṛhyasūtras.[19] The central point of these rites was that the Manes were to be well fed and this could be possible only if beef was offered to them. Therefore apart from other animals, cows and/or bulls were slain in *śrāddhas*,[20] though the degree of satisfaction they derived from them seems to have varied sometimes according to the animal offered. However, not everything depended on their choice and preference for beef was generally unquestioned. After all, the *śrāddha*, apart from being a ritual to please the ancestors, was also a feast for the community members, especially the brāhmaṇs, whose preference for beef is clearly indicated in the texts. There were several other occasions when cattle were slaughtered for the community. One of them was the *gavāmayana*, a sessional sacrifice, performed by the brāhmaṇs, culminating in an extravagant bacchanal frolicsome festival, *mahāvrata*. Similarly the *gṛhamedha*[21] was some kind of a lavish communal feast in which an unspecified number of cows were slain not in the strict ritual manner but in the crude and profane manner.[22]

Evidently then, judging by the copious textual references, not to mention the massive archaeological evidence (Jha 2002: 39–41), there is little doubt that the early Aryans in the northwestern part of the Indian subcontinent and their successors in the middle Gangetic valley slaughtered animals and cattle including the cow whose flesh they ate with great relish. Although flesh eating was forbidden for a Vedic teacher during the months between *upākarma* and *utsarjana*,[23] according to a Dharmasūtra text the flesh of cows and bulls was pure and may be eaten (*ĀpDS*, I.5.17.30-31; *VasiṣṭhaDS*, XIV.45). Not surprisingly, beef was the favourite food of the much respected sage from Mithilā, Yājñavalkya, who is said to have made the well-known statement that he would continue to eat the flesh of cows and oxen so long as it was tender (*aṃsala*),[24] though his obdurate position may also imply that already in his time an opinion against beef eating was gaining ground.

Despite all this, it has been argued that the cow was described as *aghnya* (unslayable) in the Vedic texts. The term *aghnya/aghnyā* (lit. not to be slain) has been used at four places in the *Ṛgveda* and the *Atharvaveda* "as a masculine noun equivalent to bull or ox and 42 times with a feminine ending to mean a cow."[25] Attention has also been drawn to the use of words for cow as epithet or in simile and metaphor with reference to entities of highest religious significance,[26] though these occurrences do not indicate their primary sense with reference to the actual animal. Neither of the two types of evidence adduced in favour of the "sacredness" of the Vedic cow indicates the basically unslayable character of cows. On the contrary the references seem to emphasize their economic value (Srinivasan 1979: chapter II). When slaughtered they provided food to the people and their priests and the *Śatapatha Brāhmaṇa* (XI.7.1.3) states unambiguously that "meat is the best kind of food." When milked the cows gave additional nourishment not only through milk but also through a variety of dairy products, which formed part of human diet as well as of the Vedic sacrificial oblation (*havis*). They produced oxen, which were used as draught animals. The cattle hide was used in a variety of ways. The bowstring (*jyā*) was made of a thong of cowhide—a practice that may have continued in later times (Singh 1965: 93 n. 2, 103). The different parts of the chariot were tied together with leather straps, which were also needed for binding the arrow to the shaft. The goad for driving the animals was made of cow's skin or tail. Leather strings were used for making snares as well as a kind of musical instrument called *godhā* (Srinivasan 1979: 14).[27] The utility and importance of the cattle therefore inspired warriors to fight wars (*gaviṣṭi*) for them and it is likely that part of the cattle stock of the vanquished tribes was killed during the course of the raids. All this goes against the popular notion of the inviolability of the cow throughout the Vedic period and proves that it was certainly killed for sacrifice (*yajña)* and food as well as for other requirements, notwithstanding some Atharvavedic passages, which have been interpreted as "a strong voice of protest against the slaughter of the cow" (Gopal 1959: 472).[28]

It seems likely, however, that the cow belonging to the brāhmaṇ came to acquire a certain degree of inviolability. It is known that the cow was an ideally preferred form of *dakṣiṇā*[29] (sacrificial fee) given to the brāhmaṇ priest. There are many references to the Vedic brāhmaṇ's interest in his *dakṣiṇā* (the good milch cow), and to "the dire consequences that will befall one who withholds it or injures or misappropriates it and the corresponding benefit accruing to him who bestows it" (Bloomfield 1908: 69ff; Brown 1957: 43; Shende 1985: 124; Tull 1996: 236–37). The special importance attached to the brāhmaṇ's cow, however, cannot be stretched to argue that the Vedic cow was inherently sacrosanct and unslayable, though in the later Vedic period we see the Upaniṣads questioning the efficacy of animal sacrifice as a means of achieving self-realization,[30] reading new meanings in the sacrifices, and propounding the notion of *ahiṃsā*,[31] even if some of them continued to betray a friendly attitude to the sacrificial cult.[32]

Although the Vedic and subsequent texts present divergent perceptions of ritual butchery of animals including cattle, the general Upaniṣadic idea of its futility gained in strength and may have culminated in the doctrine of *ahiṃsā*, which is the defining trait of Buddhism and Jainism. These two religions, as is well known, forcefully challenged the Vedic sacrificial slaughter of animals including the cattle and paved the way for the emergence of stable agrarian settlements, state society and other related developments (Sharma 1983: chapters V–VII) though the undermining of the Brāhmaṇical world of sacrifice did not lead to the total disappearance of cattle flesh or other meat types from the Indian dietary menu. Gautama Buddha, despite his vehement opposition to

Vedic animal sacrifice, was not averse to eating meat. He is known to have eaten beef and pork and the texts amply indicate that flesh meat very well suited the Buddhist palate. Aśoka, whose compassion for animals is undeniable, allowed certain specified animals to be killed for his kitchen. In fact, neither Asoka's list of animals exempted the cow from slaughter nor the *Arthaśāstra* of Kauṭilya specifically mentions it as unslayable. The cattle were killed for food throughout the Mauryan period. Like Buddhism, Jainism also enthusiastically took up cudgels for non-violence but it did not develop the sacred cow concept.

III

Despite the Upaniṣadic, Buddhist and Jain advocacy of *ahiṃsā*, the practice of ritual and random killing of animals including cattle continued in the post-Mauryan centuries. The law book of Manu (200 BCE–200 CE) is the most representative of the legal texts and has much to say on lawful and forbidden food, and, like the earlier law books, mentions the animals whose flesh could be eaten. Manu's list includes the porcupine, hedgehog, iguana, rhinoceros, tortoise and the hare and all those domestic animals having teeth in one jaw only, the only exception being the camel (V.18; Olivelle 2002), and it is significant that the cow is not excluded from the list of edible animals. Manu asserts that animals were created for the sake of sacrifice, that killing on ritual occasions is non-killing (V.39) and injury (*hiṃsā*) as enjoined by the Veda (*vedavihitahiṃsā*) is known to be non-injury (V.44). In the section dealing with rules for times of distress, Manu recalls the legendary examples of the most virtuous brāhmaṇs of the days of yore who ate ox-meat and dog-meat to escape death from starvation (X.105-9). Since Manu does not mention beef eating as taboo one can infer that he did not treat cow as sacrosanct—in fact the killing of cow and other cattle on ritual occasions (*madhuparka*, *śrāddha*, etc.), according to his commentator Medhātithi (ninth century), was in keeping with Vedic and post-Vedic practice.[33]

Yājñavalkya (100–300 CE), like Manu, discusses the rules regarding lawful and forbidden food. Although his treatment of the subject is less detailed, he does not differ radically from Manu's view. Yājñavalkya mentions the specific animals (deer, sheep, goat, boar, rhinoceros, etc.) and birds (e.g. partridge) whose flesh could satisfy the Manes (I.258-61). According to him a student, teacher, king, close friend and son-in-law should be offered *arghya* every year and a priest should be offered *madhuparka* on all ritual occasions (I.110). He further enjoins that a learned brāhmaṇ (*śrotriya*) should be welcomed with a big ox or goat (*mahokṣaṃ vā mahājaṃ vā śrotriyāyopakalpayet*), delicious food and sweet words (I.109). The lawgivers generally accept as lawful all those sacrifices, which, according to them, have Vedic sanction. The sacrificial slaughter of animals and domesticated bovines, as we have seen, was a Vedic practice and therefore may have been fairly common among the Brāhmaṇical circles during the early Christian centuries and even well into the later half of the first millennium CE. It would be, however, unrealistic to assume that the dharmic precept of restricting animal slaughter to ritual occasions was always taken seriously either by brāhmaṇs for whom the legal injunctions were meant or by other sections of society. It is not surprising, therefore, that Bṛhaspati (300–500 CE), while discussing the importance of local customs, says that in Madhyadeśa the artisans eat cows (*madhyadeśe karmakarāḥ śilpinaśca gavāsinaḥ*, *Bṛhaspatismṛti* 1941: 128b).

The evidence from the epics is unambiguous. While most of the characters in the *Mahābhārata* are meat eaters, it makes a laudatory reference to the king Rantideva in whose kitchen two thousand cows were butchered every day, their flesh, along with grains, being distributed among the brāhmaṇs (III.208.8-9; Sorensen 1963: 593–94). It also relates the incident in which the sage Agastya cursed king Nahuṣa and defenestrated him from the heavens for his skepticism about the Vedic injunction for the sacrifice of cows (Chakravarti 1979: 53). Similarly the *Rāmāyaṇa* of Vālmīki makes frequent reference to the killing of animals including the cow for sacrifice as well as food. Rāma was born after his father Daśaratha performed a big sacrifice involving the slaughter of a large number of animals declared edible by the Dharmaśāstras, which sanction ritual killing of the kine. Sītā, while crossing the Yamunā, assures her that she would worship her with a thousand cows and a hundred jars of wine when Rāma accomplishes his vow, though her own fondness for deer meat drives her husband crazy enough to kill Mārīca, a deer in disguise. Bharadvāja welcomes Rāma by slaughtering a fatted calf in his honour (Mitra 1969: 396). The evidence of the Sanskrit epics finds support from the earliest Buddhist Tamil epic, *Maṇimekalai* (sixth century CE?) which relates the story of one Āpputiran (lit. the son of a cow) who tried to rescue a cow from the brāhmaṇs eager to kill it for sacrifice and food (Ulrich 2007: 233–34).

Even if we leave aside the references to the therapeutic use of beef in early Indian medical literature (Jha 2002: 98–100), the continuity of the tradition of eating flesh including that of the cattle is also echoed in early Indian secular literature. The third-century Sanskrit playwright, Bhāsa, records a conversation between Rāma and Rāvaṇa in which the latter says that, among other things, cow is prescribed to be offered to the Manes (*Pratimānāṭakam*, Act V, 65). In the Gupta period, Kālidāsa alludes to the story of Rantideva who killed numerous cows every day in his kitchen (*Mehghadūta* 1979, I.48). More than two centuries later, Bhavabhūti (700 CE) refers to two instances of guest reception, which included the killing of a heifer (*Mahāvīracarita* 1973, III.2; *Uttararāmacarita* 1962, Act IV). Rājaśekhara (tenth century) mentions the practice of killing an ox or a goat in honour of a guest (*Bālarāmāyaṇa* 1984, I.38a) and Somadeva (eleventh century) narrates the story of seven brāhmaṇ boys who ate a cow (*Kathāsaritasāgara* 1960: VI.117–18). In the twelfth century Śrīharṣa mentions a variety of non-vegetarian delicacies served at a dazzling marriage feast and refers to two interesting instances of cow killing (*Naiṣadhamahākāvyam* 1981: XVII.173, 197), though in the same century the Cālukya king Someśvara indicates his preference for pork, which, despite the lawgivers' abhorrence for it, continued to be sacrificed and eaten by non-Muslims in India (Simoons 1994: 51–56; Achaya 1999: 187).[34]

IV

The above references, albeit limited in number, indicate that the ancient practice of killing the kine for food continued until at least the twelfth–thirteenth century, and there is considerable literary evidence to show that even when the practice of eating beef was strongly discouraged by brāhmaṇs and was fast falling into desuetude, its memory was preserved in later texts. For example, Jayaratha, a Kashmirian commentator (twelfth century) of the *Tantrāloka* of Abhinavagupta, cites the *Vīrāvalī Tantra* as saying that "the ancient *ṛsis* ate both beef and human flesh" (White 2003: 253). Evidence of this kind is also available from the commentaries on the kāvya literature and the earlier Dharmaśāstra texts. Among the commentators on the secular literature, Cāṇḍupaṇḍita (late thirteenth century) from Gujarat, Narahari (fourteenth century) from Telengana in Andhra Pradesh (*Naiṣadhacarita* 1965: 472) and Mallinātha (fourteenth–fifteenth century), who is associated with king Devarāya II of Vidyānagara (Vijayanagara), clearly indicate that, in earlier times, the cow was put to death for rituals and hence for food (*Naiṣadhamahākāvyam* 1981: 1137). As late as the eighteenth century Ghanaśyāma, a minister of a Tanjore ruler, states that the killing of cow in honour of a guest was the ancient rule (*Meghadūta* 1979: 83).

Similarly the authors of Dharmaśāstra commentaries and religious digests from the ninth century onwards keep alive the memory of the archaic practice of beef eating and some of them even go so far as to permit eating beef in specific circumstances. For example, Medhātithi (ninth century), probably a Kashmirian brāhmaṇ, says that a bull or ox was killed in honour of a ruler or any one deserving to be honoured and unambiguously allows eating the flesh of cow (*govyajamāṃsam*) on ritual occasions.[35] Several other writers of exegetical works seem to lend support to this view, though some times indirectly. Viśvarūpa (ninth century), a brāhmaṇ from Malwa and probably a pupil of Śaṅkara, Vijñāneśvara (eleventh century), who may have lived not far from Kalyana in modern Karnataka, Haradatta (twelfth century), also a southerner (*dakṣiṇātya*), Lakṣmīdhara (twelfth century), a minister of the Gāhaḍwāla king Govinda, Hemādri (thirteenth century), a minister of the Yādavas of Devagiri, Narasiṃha/Nṛsiṃha (fourteenth century), possibly from southern India and Mitra Miśra (seventeenth century) from Gopācala (Gwalior) support the practice of killing a cow on occasions like guest-reception and *śrāddha* in ancient times. As recently as the early twentieth century, Madana Upādhyāya from Mithilā refers to the ritual slaughter of milch cattle in the days of yore (Jha 2002: 116–21, 144). Thus even when the Dharmaśāstra commentators view cow killing with disfavour, they generally admit that it was an ancient practice and that it was to be avoided in the *kali* age, though beef eating seems to have continued among the Tāntric circles as can be inferred from a fifteenth-century text, the *Haṭhayogapradīpikā* of Svātmarāman, which lays down that the practitioner must eat the flesh of the cow (White 2003: 254).

V

While there is massive evidence of beef eating until at least the twelfth-thirteenth centuries, there is much in the normative texts to indicate that the brāhmaṇs began to discourage it from about the middle of the first millennium CE when Indian society began to be gradually feudalized leading to major socio-cultural transformation. This phase of transition, first described in the epic and Purāṇic passages as *kaliyuga*, saw many changes in the Brāhmaṇical society and modifications to its norms and customs. The Brāhmaṇical religious texts now begin to speak of many earlier practices that were forbidden in the *kaliyuga*—practices that came to be known as *kalivarjyas*. While the number of *kalivarjyas* swelled up over time, most of the relevant texts mention cow killing as forbidden in the *kali*. According to some early mediaeval lawgivers, a cow killer was an untouchable and one incurred sin even by talking to him. They increasingly associated cow slaughter and beef eating with the proliferating number of untouchable castes. It is, however, interesting that they consider the killing of cow as no more than minor behavioural aberrations like cleaning one's teeth with one's fingers and eating only salt or soil (Jha 2002: 129). Not surprisingly, one early mediaeval lawgiver Parāśara assures us that a cattle killer is bound to become pure by observing the *prājāpatya* penance and feeding the brāhmaṇs, and another prescribes, among other things, the donation of a cow presumably to a brāhmaṇ (Jha 2002: 128). None of the prescriptive texts enumerate cow killing as a major offence (*mahāpātaka*) and they provide easy escape routes by laying down expiatory procedures for intentional as well as inadvertent killing of the cow. This may imply that cattle killing may not have been uncommon in society and the atonements were prescribed merely to discourage eating cattle flesh. To what extent the Dharmaśāstric injunctions were effective, however, remains a matter of speculation.

VI

Although cow killing and beef eating gradually came to be viewed as a sin and a source of pollution from the early mediaeval period, the cow and its products (milk, curds, clarified butter, dung and urine) or their mixture called *pañcagavya* had been assuming a purificatory role from much earlier times. The Vedic texts attest to the ritual use of cow's milk and milk products, but the term *pañcagavya* occurs for the first time in the *Baudhāyana Dharmasūtra*. The law books of Manu, Viṣṇu, Vasiṣṭha, Yājñavalkya and those of several later lawgivers like Atri, Devala and Parāśara mention the use of the mixture of the five products of the cow for both purification and expiation. The commentaries and religious digests, most of which belong to the mediaeval period, abound in references to the purificatory role of the *pañcagavya*. The underlying assumption in all these cases is that the *pañcagavya* is pure. But several Dharmaśāstra texts forbid its use by women and the lower castes. If a sūdra drinks *pañcagavya*, we are told, he goes to hell (*Viṣṇusmṛti*, LIV.7; *Atrismṛti*, verse 297).

It is curious that the prescriptive texts, which repeatedly refer to the purificatory role of the cow, also provide much evidence of the notion of pollution and impurity associated with this animal. According to Manu (V.125) the food smelt by the cow has to be purified. Other early lawgivers like Viṣṇu (XXIII.38) and Yājñavalkya (I.189) also express similar views and the latter says unambiguously that while the mouth of the goat and horse is pure that of the cow is not. The notion of the impurity of the cow's mouth, reinforced by most of the later legal texts, runs counter to the ideas about the purificatory role of the cow.

It is evident from the above that the Brāhmaṇical texts abound in ambiguous and contradictory statements about the cow. But despite this the Hindutva forces have been trumpeting the idea of its sacredness and unslayability as a characteristic trait of "Hinduism." While the effectiveness of the Dharmaśāstric injunctions remains largely a matter of speculation, the possibility of at least some members of society eating beef cannot be ruled out. As recently as the late nineteenth century Swami Vivekananda was alleged to have eaten beef during his stay in America, though he strongly defended his action (Rolland 1988: 44 n. 3). Similarly in the early twentieth century Mahatma Gandhi (1927: 324) spoke of the hypocrisy of the orthodox Hindus who "do not so much as hesitate or inquire when during illness the doctor ... prescribes them beef tea."[36] Even today the practice of eating beef is quite common among the Dalits throughout the country which is why the members of upper castes in many parts of the country view it as impure and polluting. But beef is a common dietary item in most parts of north-eastern India where it is not considered a source of pollution. This is also largely true of the southernmost state of Kerala where nearly 80 per cent of the people including seventy-two Hindu communities (except the brāhmaṇs) eat beef in preference to the expensive mutton and lamb, despite the fact that the Hindutva forces have been persuading them to go easy on it (*India Today*, 15 April 1993, 72). Recent statistics of 2000 show that the meat India produces most is beef (1.44 million tonnes) and buffalo meat (1.42 million tonnes) and the per capita consumption of beef/buffalo in India is 2.8 kg, about half that of fish, but more than twice the average intake of mutton, pork and poultry. This indicates that beef eating must be quite common among meat-eaters of all religions, including the Hindus (C. R. Reddy, *The Hindu*, 16 September 2001)—a fact also supported by the surveys of butchers in different parts of the country (Bidwai, *Asia Times*, 19 August 2003).

Needless to say, then, that the image of the cow projected by Indian textual traditions, especially the Brāhmaṇical-Dharmaśāstric works, over the centuries is polymorphic. Its story through the millennia is full of inconsistencies and has not always been in conformity with dietary practices prevalent in society. It was killed and yet the killing was not killing. When it was not slain, mere remembering the old practice of butchery satisfied the brāhmaṇs. Its five products including faeces and urine have been pure but its mouth has been considered impure. Yet through these incongruous attitudes and puzzling paradoxes the Indian cow has struggled its way to sanctity and its veneration is being bandied about as a characteristic trait of "Hinduism" though she has failed to achieve the status of a goddess and earn a temple in her honour (Basham 1996: 319). On the contrary the cow is often found bumbling between the luxurious limos of the privileged and the pushcarts of the poor, causing traffic snarls in Indian metros, and browsing on heaps of garbage, ranging from inedible throw-outs to the stinking carrion. The holiness of the cow is thus elusive—as elusive as Hindu identity itself!

Notes

Introduction

1. Since the caste system (*varṇāśramadharma*) has always occupied a central position in the orthodox Sanatanist Hindu religion, and since the Arya Samajist ideology preached the necessity to recognize merit-based caste and not the traditional hereditary caste system, questions were raised about how a convert could be looked upon as a Hindu unless he or she was assigned a place in the caste hierarchy. This added a controversial dimension to *śuddhi* (reconversion) but in the early twentieth century, leaders like Madan Mohan Malaviya lent support to this movement (Jaffrelot 2007: 68–69).

2. The word "Hindutva" was first mentioned by Pancānana Tarkartana in 1840 in the context of the debate generated by John Muir.

3. This portrayal of Muslims, however, was contested by intellectuals like Bhudev Mukhopadhyaya (1827–94) and others (Hasan 1996: 201).

4. Bal Gangadhar Tilak authored several books, the most well-known of them being the *Orion or Researches into the Antiquity of the Vedas* (1893), *Arctic Home in the Vedas* (1903) and the *Gitarahsya* (1915).

5. Some years ago the RSS and the Hindu right-wing parties tried to dissociate themselves from Golwalkar's book, though without success (Shamsul Islam 2006: 44–52).

1. Deconstructing Hindu Identity

1. For a rebuttal of Lal, see Sharma 1999b: 35–45; Habib 2001: 65–92.

2. For an assessment of the "evidence" of horse in the Harappan context, see Sharma 1994: 14–34; idem 1999a: 12–21; Parpola 1994: 155–59. For the debate centring on the forged evidence of the horse, see Witzel and Farmer 2000.

3. For detailed comments on the views of B. B. Lal and his followers, see Guha 2005: 399–426. In keeping with his indigenist approach, Lal (1960: 4–24) speaks of the resemblance between the graffiti on megalithic and chalcolithic pottery on the one hand and Harappan script characters and Brāhmī letters on the other. More recently he has made a tongue-in-cheek endorsement of the view that the Harappan script was the precursor of the later Brāhmī (2002: 132–35), though not long ago he was of the view that the Harappan script was read from right to left. The most recent view, however, is that the Harappans may not have been a literate people at all (Farmer and Witzel 2004: 19–57).

4. This is the only Ṛgvedic passage where the word *saptasindhava* is

used in the sense of territory; at all other places in the *Ṛgveda* it is used to mean the seven rivers (*Vedic Index*, II.424).

5. According to the *Kauṣītaki Upaniṣad* (II.13), Āryāvarta was bounded on the west by Adarsana near Kurukṣetra and on the east by Kālakavana near Allahabad.

6. For a discussion of the Tamil mother and Bhāratamātā, see Sumathi Ramaswamy 2003: 551–68.

7. A *yojana* is a measure of distance equal to four *krośas* or eight or nine miles (V. S. Apte, *Practical Sanskrit English Dictionary*, sv. *yojanam*).

8. According to some it is divided into six parts (*khaṇḍas*), of which one is *āryakhaṇḍa* and is the same as Bhārata, the remaining five being *mleccha-khaṇḍas*. Among the Jain texts, the *Jambūddivpaññattisuttam* provides the most detailed account of Jambūdvīpa and Bhārata. The Jain texts had several geographical categories in common with the Purāṇic ones, but they had many unique spatio-temporal conceptions too.

9. Historians who locate Indian nationalism in the distant past are, to a certain extent, inspired by the champions of the notion of a Greater India in ancient times. An organization called the Greater India Society was founded in Calcutta in 1926 with the objective of promoting the study of the history and culture of Asian countries in which ancient Indians supposedly established colonies. Rabindranath Tagore was its *purodha* (spiritual head), but scholars who extended active support to the Society included P. C. Bagchi, Suniti Kumar Chatterji, Phanindra Nath Bose, Kalidas Nag, U. N. Ghoshal, Nalinaksha Datta and R. C. Majumdar (Bayly 2004: 703–44). It is the last named historian (R. C. Majumdar), to whose writings Hindu supremacists and cultural nationalists often turn for legitimacy even today. Moreover, there were and still are scholars in different parts of the country who feed into the "Greater India" dialectic. One of them, Raghuvira, made the following statement: "Our ignorant journalists and governmental papers call Indonesia "Hindesia," as though the term were to be divided into "India" and "Asia" (Hind + Asia). The fools! The correct translation of Indonesia is *bharatadvipa*, for *nesia* derives from the Greek *nesos*, island" (Bharati 1970: 276).

10. Among those who, directly or indirectly, support the idea of the Harappan religion as being the "progenitor" of modern "Hinduism," mention may be made of Parpola (1994), Chakrabarti (1999), and Lal (1997, 2002). S. P. Gupta, in a book review, makes the following fantastic assertion: "the culture of the Indus-Saraswati...continues to live in India even today" (2000–2001, *Puratattva* 31: 189). For a reasoned critique of their views, see Shrimali 2003: 1–59; Guha 2005: 399–426.

11. The history textbooks used in the RSS-run Shishu Mandirs and other schools abound in similar pearls of wisdom about Hinduism.

12. Arvind Sharma (2002: 6) points out that Muḥammad ibn Qāsim appointed his adversary Dahir's minister Siakar as his advisor after the latter's acceptance of Islam. Since conversion from what he calls "Hindu religion" became possible, he seems to imply that a Hindu identity had already emerged. Similarly, the Brāhmaṇ princes of Sind, Jaysiyah b. Dahir and his brother Sassah, converted to Islam at the invitation of the Caliph 'Umar b. 'Abd al-Aziz (Maclean 1989: 33, 48). But mere acceptance of Islam by certain

Sindis does not justify a reified perception of Hinduism as early as the eighth century.

13. Several Arab travellers and geographers refer to the existence of large numbers of religious sects in India. For example, Ibn Khurdādbih (ninth century) refers to the existence of forty-two sects among the people of India (Lawrence 1976: 20) and al-Gandizi, a contemporary of Alberuni, tells us that the Indians were divided into ninety-nine religious communities (Friedmann 1975: 216).

14. Indian idolatry received much attention from the twelfth-century Muslim heresiographer al-Shahrastānī, who wrote on both Muslim and non-Muslim sects. Of the four categories of religious groups known to him, an important one was the group of "the ancient as well as the materialist philosophers, the star- and idol worshippers and the Brahmans" (Lawrence 1976: 17). Although he shows a remarkable empathy for the Indian sects he asserts that they are in the final analysis polytheists (Friedmann 1975: 214; Lawrence 1976: 277).

15. The fact that Alberuni used the word "Hindu" in the religious sense has been contested by Syed Farid Alatas according to whom the term does not occur in the Arabic text and the word "hind" which finds mention in it does not have a religious connotation (Alatas 2008: 16).

16. For a detailed though biased view of Alberuni's perception of Brāhmaṇical religion, see Arvind Sharma 1983.

17. The general absence of an essentialist view of the religion of the Hindus may be inferred from the many inscriptions including the one from Veraval, discussed by Anwar Hussain (1993, chapter IV). B. D. Chattopadhyaya (1998: 78) rightly points out that whatever essentialism may be there in Alberuni's description is contradicted by many records including the Veraval inscription, which speaks of the reconstruction of a demolished mosque by Jayasiṃha Siddharāja.

18. The Moroccan traveller Ibn Battūtah, a contemporary of Baranī, interpreted the name Hindu Kush as "Hindu killer" because the Indian slaves passing through its mountainous terrain perished in the snows. This has been given a communal slant by Arvind Sharma (2002: 9).

19. The author of the *Dabistān* has been variously identified, e.g. as "Mobad," Muhsin Fani, Mirza Zulfiqar Beg and Kaikhusrau Isfandyar.

20. Also see n. 16 above.

21. The pandits were Somanātha (Subāji Bāpu), Haracandra Tarkapancānana and Nilakaṇṭha Goreh, the last of whom ultimately converted to Christianity and was baptized as Nehemiah Goreh. The material produced in the context of the controversy has been discussed by Richard Fox Young (1981).

22. The multi-volume lexicon *Śabdakalpadruma* by Rādhākānta Deb appeared between 1819 and 1858 and the *Vācaspatyam* by Tārānātha Tarkavācaspati was published in 1873.

23. The crucial passage is given by V. S. Apte (*Practical Sanskrit English Dictionary*, sv. *hindu*): *hindudharmapraloptāro jāyante cakravarttinaḥ/hīnam ca dūṣayatyeka hinduritiucyate priye*. Apte dates the text to the eighth century CE, but one is intrigued by its reference to *tāntriks* born in London who will become lords of the earth!

24. *hīnam dūṣayati iti hindu*: the Hindu "spoils" (*dūṣayati*) what is "inferior" (*hīnam*) (Halbfass 1990: 515 n. 96). The twentieth-century text *Dharmapradīpa*, written by three leading pandits in the 1930s (Calcutta, 1937), discusses in detail the rules laid down for the purification of those Hindus who joined or were forced to join other religions: *atra kevalaṃ balād eva mlecchadharmaṃ svīkāritānāṃ hindūnām...vividhāḥ prāyaścittavidhayo nirdiṣṭā dṛśyante*, p. 219 cited in Halbfass 1990: 534 n. 66. The word also occurs in the *Dharmatattvavinirṇaya* by Vāsudeva Śāstrin Abhyaṅkara (Poona, 1929).

25. David N. Lorenzen 1999: 630–59; idem 1996, "Introduction."

26. Charles Grant used the term "Hindooism" first in a letter to John Thomas in 1787 and subsequently in his *Observations on the State of Society among the Subjects of Great Britain*, written in 1792 (Sweetman 2003: 56 n. 12). William Jones also used the term "Hindu" in the religious sense in 1787 (Mukherjee 1968: 119; Killingley 2003: 513). Rammohun Roy was, however, perhaps "the first Hindu" to use the word "Hindooism" in 1816 (Killingley 1993: 60 cited in Richard King 1999: 100).

27. Several scholars have argued that Hinduism was a colonial construct which finally took shape when the imperial administration engaged in the classification into categories of the Indian people through the mechanism of the census. Important among them are Vasudha Dalmia (1995: 176–210); Frykenberg (1997: 82–107); Hawley (1991: 20–32); Harjot Oberoi (1994: 16–17); and Heinrich von Stietencron (1997: 32–53). Their views have been contested by quite a few scholars in recent years, e.g. Sweetman (2003) and Pennington (2005). Their main source of inspiration is David Lorenzen (1999: 631) who has argued that "a Hindu religion...acquired a much sharper self-conscious identity through the rivalry between Muslims and Hindus in the period between 1200 and 1500, and was firmly established before 1800" (631). While he thus assigns primary agency to "rivalry between Muslims and Hindus" in the construction of Hinduism, he also pronounces: "Hinduism wasn't invented by anyone, European or Indian. Like Topsy, it just grow'd" (655). One wonders if this recourse to escapism is not a mere muddying of the waters of history.

28. Recently Brian K. Pennington (2005) has vehemently opposed the view that Britain invented Hinduism on the grounds, first, that that argument "grants...too much power to colonialism" and, second, that denying the existence of Hinduism prior to the arrival of the British "introduces an almost irreparable disruption in Indian traditions that can only alienate contemporary Indians from their own traditions" (5). He seems to forget that colonialisms everywhere have manipulated facts to suit their interests. Worse, must historians cease to work because their reasoned conclusions show that "traditions," held to be crucial to the psychic welfare of today's people, are concocted?

29. The only clarity about Hinduism is that it is used as a catch-all category for all non-Abrahamaic religions and is thus a negative appellation. In the Hindu Marriage Act (1955), "Hindu" includes not only Buddhists, Jains and Sikhs but also all those who are not Muslims, Christians, Parsees or Jews. There is therefore much substance in Frits Staal's view that no meaningful notion of Hinduism can be obtained except by exclusion, and in his argument it fails to qualify both as a religion and as "a meaningful unit of discourse" (1989: 397).

30. It is not surprising that early twentieth-century pandits like Vāsudev Śastrin Abhyaṅkara, Anantakṛṣṇa Śāstri, Sītārām Śāstri and Śrīvijaya Bhattā-charya were against the introduction of "new sectarian traditions" (*nūtanasampradāya*, *Dharmapradīpa* 1937: 64) and described themselves as "followers of eternal religion" (*sanātanadharmīya*, *sanātanadharmāvalambin*, *Dharmapradīpa* 1937: 207, 219: *Dharmatattvavinirṇaya*, pp. 39ff.). See Halbfass 1990: 260.

31. It has been suggested that the word *sanātana* may have some connection with *sanatā*, which occurs in the Vedic literature only twice. At one place it occurs along with *dharma* (*ṚV* 3.3.1d) and at another, without it (*ṚV* 2.3.6ab). In both cases the word *sanatā* means "from old times" or "always." I am thankful to Professor Shingo Einoo, who drew my attention to these references.

32. *Mahābhārata*, xii.96.13; 128.30; 131.2; xiii.44.32; 96.46; xiv.50.37; cited in Halbfass 1990: 558 n. 56.

33. According to the story, when his mother was being led away by a brāhmaṇ, he flew into a rage and was calmed down by his father, who told him not to get angry because this was the eternal law (*eṣa dharmaḥ sanātanaḥ*), *Mahābhārata*, I.113, verses 11-14.

34. *Sanātanadharma: An Elementary Text-book of Hindu Religion and Ethics* (Central Hindu College, Benares, 1910). This was followed by several works on the *sanātanadharma*, e.g., *Sanātanadharmadīpikā* by Haṃsayogin (Madras, 1917); Ganga Prasad, *The Fountainhead of Religion* (1909, reprint San Diego: The Book Tree, 2000); Shri Bharat Dharma Mahamandala, ed., *The World's Eternal Religion* (Benares, 1920); etc.

35. *Bhāgavata Purāṇa* 1.2.3, 1.3.42, 12.13.15; *Nāradīya Purāṇa* 1.1.36, 1.9.97; *Skanda Purāṇa* 5.3.1.22 cited in Smith 1989: 26.

36. The first edition of the Tamil translation of the Bible by the Lutheran missionary B. Ziegenbalg, which appeared in 1714, was entitled *Vedapustagam* (Veda Book) and he described both the Bible and the Christian religion as the true Veda (*satyavedam*). Similarly a Sanskrit catechism written by the French Jesuit priest Calmette was called *Satyavedasārasaṃgraha* (Halbfass 1990: 340).

37. Although it is not possible to discuss here the various forms and levels of atheism and heresies in India, it is necessary to recall that among those who repudiated the authority of the Vedas outside the Brāhmaṇical fold and earned the epithets *pāṣandas* (heretics) and *nāstikas* (non-believers in the Vedas), the important ones are the Jains, the Buddhists and the Cārvākas, the followers of Cārvāka also known as *lokāyatikas*. The Vedas, according to the Jains, were *anāryavedas*, which they replaced with their own scriptures, calling them *āryavedas*. They also describe the Vedas as *mithyāsūtras* (*micchāsūya*) (Renou 1965: 87). Gautama Buddha is equally unsparing in his denunciation of the Vedas and says that "the talk of the Brāhmaṇas versed in the three Vedas turns out to be ridiculous, mere words, a vain and empty thing" (*Dīghanikāya*, I, Tevijjasutta 15). Further, he describes the three Vedas as "foolish talk," "a waterless desert," and their threefold wisdom as "a pathless jungle" and "a perdition" (ibid.). The strongest condemnation of the Vedic texts, however, came from the Cārvākas. According to them the Veda is

"tainted with the three faults of untruth, self-contradiction, and tautology...the incoherent rhapsodies of knaves" (*dhurtapralāpa*) (*Sarva-darśaṇa-saṇgraha* 1914: 4).

38. A sceptical view of the Vedic sacrifice is found in *Ṛ̣V*, V.30.1, VI.18.3, VI.27.3, VIII.64.7, VIII.100.3, X.22.1 (Heesterman 1985: 225). Also see Doniger 1971: 283 n. 83.

39. Sarup (1984: 74–75) lists several anti-Vedic Upaniṣadic passages: *Muṇḍaka Up.*, III.2.3; *Kaṭha Up.*, I.2.23; *Bṛh. Up.*, I.5.23; *Kauṣītaki Up.*, II.5; *Chāndogya Up.*, V.11–24; *Taittirīya Up.*, II.5.

40. The *Mahānirvāṇatantra* is "probably the most widely known" and the most recent of the Tantras. Written in the second half of the eighteenth century, it contains much material on such varied themes as marriage, conjugal ethics, inheritance, caste rules and slavery, though according to one view it was a "well-intentioned fraud" (J. D. M. Derrett 1977: 197–242; Teun Goudriaan and Sanjukta Gupta 1981: 98–101; Bhattacharyya 1982: 74–75).

41. The smārtas, who joined the Vīraśaiva movement in large numbers, retained their superiority, undermined its fraternalism and paved the way for the growth of the Brāhmaṇical caste system among its followers. Not surprisingly, the Vīraśaivas, in the later phase of their movement, preached loyalty to the *varṇāśramadharma*, as is evident from the works of Bhīmakavi and Śrīpati Paṇḍita (both of the fourteenth century). The latter even said that only the performance of caste duties and Vedic rites could purify a person and prepare him for final liberation (Nandi 2000: 477; Jaiswal 1991: 22). The Vīraśaiva emphasis on the observance of caste duties as well as on the necessity of seeking legitimation from the Vedas is evident from one of their basic texts, the *Liṇgadhāraṇacandrikā* (Renou 1965: 61 n. 1).

42. Among the younger Indian scholars advocating the idea of *sui generis* religion, mention may be made of Kunal Chakrabarti, according to whom "religion as man's response to the ultimate reality has an autonomy and a dynamic of its own" (1995: 189).

43. Constraints of space do not permit us to list and discuss all the recent writings on Hinduism, but a few of the most recent ones may be mentioned: Flood 2003, 2004; Arvind Sharma 2003; and Mittal and Thursby 2004.

44. Unlike most scholars of religion, there are a few who have looked at early Indian religious developments against the backdrop of social change. Examples are Debiprasad Chattopadhyaya (1959), D. D. Kosambi (1962), Suvira Jaiswal (1981), R. S. Sharma (1974) and R. N. Nandi (1986). For comments on their relevant writings, see Kunal Chakrabarti 1995: 182–89.

2. Tolerant Hinduism: Evidence and Stereotype

1. *Varāhpurāṇa* 4.2; *Matsyapurāṇa* 285.6–7; *Agnipurāṇa* 49.8; *Bhāgavatapurāṇa* X.40.22 and I.3 cited in John Clifford Holt (2004: 15). In his interesting study Holt demonstrates that while Brāhmaṇism accorded the Buddha the status of an *avatāra* of Viṣṇu in India, Buddhists in Sri Lanka incorporated Viṣṇu in their religious culture.

2. The "merger" of Buddhists in the Brāhmaṇical social order and the consequent transformation of Buddhism has been discussed in some detail by Chakrabarti (2001: chapter IV) and Sircar (1971: chapter XII).

3. *Tattvasaṃgraha* of Śāntarakṣita, ed. Dwarkadas Shastri (Varanasi: Bauddha Bharati, 1968); Eng. trans. Ganganatha Jha, Gaekwad Oriental Series (Baroda, 1937).

3. Holy Cow: Elusive Identity

1. In *Ṛ̣V*, I.162, 163, the details of the horse sacrifice are available for the first time.

2. *Gosava* was a kind of cow sacrifice which, according to the *Mahābhārata* (3.30.17), should not be performed in the Kali age. See V. S. Apte, *The Practical Sanskrit-English Dictionary*, s.v. *gosava*. According to *TB*, II.7.6, one who desires *svarājya* should perform this sacrifice. The *ĀpDS* states that for a year after performing *gosava* the sacrificer should be *paśuvrata* (act like cattle), i.e., should drink water like them and cut grass (with his teeth) and even have sexual relations with his mother: *teneṣṭvā saṃvatsaraṃ paśuvrato bhavati/upāvahāyodakaṃ pivettṛṇāni cācchindyāt/upa mataramiyādupa svasāramupa sagotrāṃ*, XXII.12.12-20; 13.1-3, cited in Kane 1974: II, pt. 2, 1213 n. 2644. Also see Thite 1975: 97–100.

3. Mitra (1969: I, 363) also cites a passage from the *Tāṇḍya Brāhmaṇa* of the *Sāmaveda* which recommends cattle of different colours for each successive year.

4. Monier-Williams, *Sanskrit-English Dictionary*, *s.v. paśu*. Cf. Macdonell and Keith 1958: I, 580–82. The Sanskrit *paśu* = Avestan *pasu* means domestic animals, livestock and sacrificial animals but it also frequently indicates simply cattle as the domestic animal and the sacrificial animal par excellence (Lincoln 1982: 65 and n. 98). Also see Mayrhofer, *A Concise Etymological Dictionary*, II, s.v. *paśuḥ*.

5. Kane 1974: II, pt. 2, 1224; Thite 1975: 83–9. Also see 'animal' in the index to Kolhatkar (1999).

6. *TS*, VI.3.10.2-6; *Gopatha Brāhmaṇa* (*Pūrvabhāga*), I.3.18. For a detailed description see also Naoshiro Tsuji (alias Fukushima) 1952: 87–100; Mitra 1969: I, 373–74; Malamoud 1996: 169–80. For references to sacrificial animals as food see *ŚB*, III.2.1.12; V.2.1.16; VII.5.2.42; VIII.3.1.13, VIII.3.3.2-4, VIII.5.2.1, VIII.6.2.1, 13; IX.2.3.40. Also *TB*, III.9.8.3.

7. Renou (1971: 114) and Mitra (1969: I, 363) have interpreted *śūlagava* as a sacrifice of "spitted ox" or roast beef. The word *śūla* is found in the *Ṛgveda* only once, but it occurs more often in the later Brāhmaṇas (Renou 1971: 114; Mitra 1969: I, 363ff.). Cf. Kane 1974: II, pt. 2, 831–32; Gonda 1980: 435–37.

8. Geldner interprets the word as "cows which bring guests" in his translation of *Ṛ̣V*, X.68.3 (Geldner 1951: 244) and so does Oldenberg (1912: 272). That the word is usually understood as "(a cow) which brings guests" is also clear from Mayrhofer, *Etymologisches Wörterbuch des Altindoarischen*, I, s.v. *atithi*.

9. Macdonell and Keith 1958: II, 145; Kane 1974: II, pt. 2, 749–56. The epithet Atithigva is also often used for the Ṛgvedic chief Divodāsa and has been interpreted by Bloomfield as "he who (always) has a cow for a guest" (Jha 2002: 50 n. 65).

10. *AB*, III.4, cited in Kane 1974: II, pt. 1, 542 n. 1254. Also see *ŚB*, III.4.1.2 according to which an ox or a goat was cooked for a guest, a king or a brāhmaṇ.

11. That the cow was offered to the guest of honour is mentioned in most of the Gṛhyasūtra texts but, according to the *ĀśGS*, the animal was slain only after he ordered its immolation with the words "*Om kuru*" (accomplish, Om). Shingo Einoo has provided a very useful table showing the procedures of *madhuparka* and indicating the specific Sūtra passages which refer to the killing of the cow in honour of guests (Einoo 1996: 83–84).

12. *ĀśGS*, I.24.1-33; *PārGS*, I.3.1-31; *KhādiraGS*, IV.4.5-23; *GobhGS* IV.10.26; *HirGS*, I.4.12-13; *ĀpGS*, V.13.1-20. Cf. *ĀpDS* (V.IV.8), which expressly provides for the offering of cow's flesh as a great delicacy to distinguished brāhmaṇ and kṣatriya guests (Banerji 1962: 157 n. 39). Also see Kane 1974: II, pt. 2, 542; Keith 1970: 374.

13. There is textual evidence to indicate that the *madhuparka* rite was observed more than once in the course of marriage ceremonies. Āpastamba, for example, lays down that a cow should be killed for the bridegroom and another for those revered by him and Śāṅkhyāyana speaks of two *madhuparka* cows in marriage. *ĀpGS*, I.3.5-8; *ŚāṅkhGS*, I.12.10.

14. The word *goghna* has sometimes been interpreted to mean a "cow killer." Going by the commentary *Kāśikāvṛtti* on Pāṇini, however, the word does not literally mean a "cow-killer" but refers to a guest for whom a cow is killed to prepare a meal (Madhav Deshpande in an email message dated 18 June 2004 to the Y-Indology List).

15. The Vedic texts and the post-Vedic sūtra literature provide numerous references to the ritual use of the hide of a cow or a bull. Interestingly the soma plant was pressed on the cow's or bull's hide to extract its juice.

16. *atha ya icchet putro me paṇḍito vigītaḥ, samitiṃ-gamaḥ, śuśrūṣtāṃ vācaṃ bhāṣitā jāyeta, sarvān vedān anubruvita, sarvam āyur iyād iti, māṃsodanaṃ pācayitvā sarpiṣmantaṃ aśnīyātām; īsvarau janayita vai, aukṣṇena vārṣabheṇa vā*, *Bṛ. Up.*, VI.4.18.

17. *AV*, XII.2, 48 cited in Keith and Macdonell 1958, *s.v. agni-dagdha.*

18. *KauśS*, 81, 20-29; *ĀśGS*, IV.3.19-21; *KauśGS*, V.2.13; V.3.1-5, etc. cited in Gopal 1959: 360–61; Kane 1974: IV, 189–266. The animal killed at the time of cremation was called *anustaraṇī*, which, according to Kane (1974: IV, 206 n. 486), means either a cow or a female-goat. But V. S. Apte interprets it as a cow sacrificed at the funeral ceremony (*The Practical Sanskrit–English Dictionary*, s.v. *anustaraṇam*). A suggestion has also been made that the *anustaraṇīni* cow is "normally one that has not calved" (Brown 1957: 33 n. 17).

19. The word *śrāddha* (ceremony in honour and benefit of the dead but different from the funeral ceremony) is not found in the Vedic texts and, according to Kane (1974: IV, 350), it first occurs in the *Kaṭhopaniṣad* (1.3.17). But it comes to occupy a very important place in the Dharmaśāstra literature and

more than fifteen specialized treatises devoted to the procedures of *śrāddha* were produced in mediaeval times.

20. According to *ĀpDS*, II.7.16.25: "the Manes derive very great pleasure from the flesh of cow" (Banerji 1962: 157). According to the *PārGS*, on the eleventh day after the death, the relatives of the dead should feed an odd number of brāhmaṇs a meal with meat; it adds that a cow could also be immolated in honour of the dead. *HirGS*, II.15.1; *BaudhGS*, II.11.51; *VaikhGS*, IV.3; *ĀpGS*, VIII.22.3-4.

21. For references to the *gṛhamedha* and its discussion see Heesterman (1993: 190–93, 200–202).

22. Heesterman argues that in the case of *gṛhamedha*, the word used for cow slaughter is derived from the root *han* (to kill) which is different from the ritualistic killing indicated in the Vedic sacrifices by the term *ālambhana* (1993: 189–201).

23. Kane 1974: II, pt. 2, 777. The terms *upākarma* and *utsarjana* refer to the beginning and cessation of Vedic studies.

24. *tasmāddhenvanaḍuhornāśnīyāt/tadu hovāca yājñavalkyaḥ/aśnāmyevāhaṃ māṃsalam cedbhavatiti/ ŚB*, III.1.2.21 in Kane 1974: II, pt. 2, 773. The exact meaning of the word *aṃsala* is controversial. It has generally been translated as "tender" but, according to Michael Witzel, it might as well mean "fatty" (Witzel 1991: 9–20).

25. Brown 1957: 33. Kane (1974: II, pt. 2, 772–3) also cites Vedic passages mentioning the word *aghnyā*. Cf. Proudfoot 1987: 14.

26. Macdonell (1963: 150–1) makes the valid point that the cow entered the conceptions of Vedic mythology—a view repeated by him and Keith (1958: II, 146). But on Macdonell's own admission, this was owing to the great utility of the cow. For a convincing refutation of the above view see Brown (1957).

27. Cowhide has continued to be used for various purposes throughout Indian history and it is used even now in India in making the *mridangam*—the double-headed leather drum—without which the Carnatic musical tradition of southern India is unthinkable (Anand 2003).

28. Gopal treats *AV* XII.4.38, 53 and XII.5.36-37 as a protest against the killing of the cow. In our view, however, these passages indicate that the Vedic texts contained ideas that did not favour ritual killing of the kine and may be taken, at best, to suggest that the Vedic tradition was not monolithic.

29. Etymologically the word *dakṣiṇā* is so called because it imparts power or strength to the receiver (Apte, *The Practical Sanskrit–English Dictionary*, s.v. *dakṣiṇā*). It is used in the sense of a good milch cow or "the richly milking one" in the Vedic texts because it gave wealth and hence strength to the priest (Thite 1975: 151–61; Proudfoot 1987: 3, 185 n. 22).

30. That the Upaniṣadic position on sacrifice was different from that of the Vedic texts is clear from many passages (e.g. *Br. Up.*, 1.4.10; 3.9.6; 3.9.21; *Ch. Up.*, 1.10-12; 4.1-3) to which attention has been drawn by several scholars like Paul Deussen (1906) and A. B. Keith (1970). More recently this point has been touched upon, albeit briefly, by Thapar (1996: 11–27).

31. The word *ahiṃsā/ahiṃsāyai* finds mention in several later Vedic and post-Vedic texts e.g. *AV*, *TS*, *MS*, *Kāṭhaka Saṃhitā*, *Kapiṣṭhala Kaṭha Saṃhitā*, *AB*, *TA*, *SB* (for reference to specific passages see Vishva Bandhu,

A Vedic Word-Concordance, Vishveshvaranand Vedic Research Institute, Hoshiarpur, I, pt. 1 (1976) and II, pt. 1 (1973), s.v. *ahiṃsā*). But there is a wide divergence of scholarly opinion on the origin of the idea of non-violence (*ahiṃsā*). According to Ludwig Alsdorf (1962) the doctrine of *ahiṃsā* originated in the Indus Valley—a view which, it has been pointed out, pushes "the problem out of sight, into the limbo of an as yet undeciphered past." According to Hans-Peter Schmidt (1968: 653) the word *ahiṃsā* first occurs in the sense of a new doctrine in the teachings of Ghora Āṅgīrasa found in *Ch. Up.*, III.17.4. Like Schmidt, Heesterman (1984: 120) locates the origin of the doctrine within the Vedic-Brāhmaṇical tradition. Independent of these scholars, however, Witzel (1991) has asserted that the "origin of *ahiṃsā* lies in the horror of killing and in this sense non-violence is a selfish action, not altruism and love for all beings...a prudent action taken in one's own interest...not necessarily a Jaina, Buddhist or an 'aboriginal' development at all, but which has its roots in much earlier Brāhmaṇical thought." In spite of the divergent opinions about the origin of *ahiṃsā*, there is a strong opinion in favour of the śramaṇa traditions as being its source (Brown 1966: 56; Dumont 1988: 150; Smith 1990: 198).

32. The *Kaṭhopaniṣad* (I.1.1) tells us that Vājaśrava performed the Viśvajit sacrifice for worldly gains, and the *Śvetāśvatara Upaniṣad* (II.6) extols the fire offering. Similarly, the *Maitrāyaṇīya Upaniṣad* also speaks of the importance of sacrifice (I.1) and of the knowledge of the Vedas (VII.8-10).

33. *govyajamāṃsamaprokṣitaṃbhakṣayedàmadhupākṛtānāmevāsadrūpama nūdyate*: Medhātithi on Manu, V.27; *madhuparkovyākhyātaḥ tatra govadhavihitaḥ*: Medhātithi on Manu, V.41; see *Mānava-Dharma-Śāstra*, 1886, ed. V. N. Mandalik, 604, 613.

34. James Tod (1829: I, 451–2), writing in the early nineteenth century, reports the hunting and eating of wild boar among various groups including the Rajputs. However, the anti-pig sentiment, traceable to pre-Islamic times in West Asia, has been very strong among Indian Muslims, though certain Islamic groups in Mauritania, Morocco, Algeria, Tunisia, Kurdistan and Indonesia permit pork. Interestingly, the two Persian doctors, Avicenna and Haly Abbas, spoke favarourably of pork as food (Simoons 1994: 35, 341, nn. 180–82).

35. See n. 33 above.

36. In this context, Gandhi also refers to a five-footed "miraculous" cow which he saw at the Kumbha Mela at Allahabad in 1915, the fifth foot being nothing but "a foot cut off from a live calf and grafted upon the shoulder of the cow" which attracted the lavish charity of the ignorant Hindu (1927: 325). Another example of the false pretence of piety is seen in the practice of fooka, which is a painful method of stimulation to extend the milk-giving period of the cow (Margul 1968: 69).

Bibliography

Abhidhānacintāmaṇi. 1964. Edited with an introduction by Nemichandra Sastri, with the Hindi commentary *Maṇiprabhā* by Haragovind Sastri. Varanasi: Chowkhamba.

Achaya, K. T. 1999. *A Historical Dictionary of Indian Food.* New Delhi: Oxford University Press.

Agnipurāṇa. 1987. Pune: Anandashrama Sanskrit Press.

Agrawal, Vasudev Sharan. 1958. *Kādambarī: Ek Sāṃskritik Adhyayan.* Varanasi: Chowkhamba.

——1963. *India as Known to Pāṇini.* 2nd edn. Varanasi: Prithvi Prakashan.

——1964. *Harṣacarita: Ek Sāmskritik Adhyāyan.* Patna: Bihar Rashtra Bhasha Parisad.

Ahmad, Qeyamuddin. 1982. "Baranī's References to the Hindus in the *Tārīkh-i-Fīrūzshāhī* Territorial and Other Dimensions." *Islamic Culture,* LVI: 295–302.

Aitareya Brāhmaṇa. 1879. Ed. Theodor Aufrecht and A. Marcus. Bonn; Eng. trans. 1971, A. B. Keith, *Rigveda Brāhmaṇas: The Aitareya and Kauṣītaki Brāhmaṇas of the Rigveda.* Harvard University Press. 1st Indian reprint, Delhi: Motilal Banarsidass.

Alam, Ishrat. 2005. "Names for India in Ancient Indian Texts and Inscriptions." In Irfan Habib, ed., *India: Studies in the History of an Idea.* Delhi: Munshiram Manoharlal.

Alatas, Syed Farid. 2008. "Intellectual and Structural Challenges to Academic Dependency." Keynote Address: *ADRI-SEPPHIS Seminar on Coping with Academic Dependency: How?* Patna.

Ali, S. M. 1966. *The Geography of the Purāṇas.* New Delhi: Peoples Publishing House.

Alsdorf, Ludwig. 1962. *Beträge zur Geschichte von Vegetarismus und Rinderverehrung in Indien.* Wiesbaden: Akademie der Wissenschaften and der Literatur.

Amarakośa. 1913. Ed. Krishnaji Govind Oka, as *The Nāmalingānuśāsana: Amarakośa of Amarasiṃha* (with the commentary of Kṣīrasvāmin). Poona: Law Printing Press. Delhi: Upasana Prakashana, 1981.

Anand, S. 2003. "Thyagaraja's Cow." *Outlook* (8 October).

Āpastamba Dharmasūtra. 1932. Ed. G. Buhler. Bombay: Bombay Sanskrit Series. Eng. trans. G. Buhler. SBE II. Oxford, 1879.

Āpastamba Gṛhyasūtra. 1971. Ed. Umesh Chandra Pandey. Varanasi: Chowkhmaba. Eng. trans. G. Buhler. SBE II. Oxford, 1879.

Apte, V. S. 1998. *The Practical Sanskrit-English Dictionary.* Revised and enlarged edition. Kyoto: Rinsen Book Co.

Arthaśāstra of Kauṭilya. 1997. Ed. and trans. R. P. Kangle. *The Kauṭīlīya Arthaśāstra.* 3 parts, 2nd edn. Reprint, Delhi: Motilal Banarsidass.

Aṣṭādaśasmṛtyaḥ Saka. 1846. Ed. with Hindi trans. Sundarlal Tripathi. Bombay: Khemraj Shrikrishnadas.

Aṣṭādhyāyī of Pāṇiṇi. 1962. Ed. and trans. Srisa Chandra Vasu. Delhi: Motilal Banarsidass.

Āśvalāyana Gṛhyasūtra. 1978. New edition. Poona: Ānandāśramasamskritgrānthāvali 105. Eng. trans. H. Oldenberg. SBE XXIX. Oxford, 1886.

Atharva Veda. 1924. Ed. R. Roth, W. D. Whitney and Max Lindenau. Berlin: F. Dummler. Eng. trans. M. Bloomfield, *Hymns of the Atharvaveda.* SBE XLII. Oxford, 1897.

Ātmatattvaviveka of Udayanācārya. 1995. Ed. N. S. Dravid. Shimla: Indian Institute of Advanced Study.

Āyārāṅgasutta (Ācārāngasūtra). 1910. Ed. W. S. Schubring. Leipzig: F. A. Brockhaus. Eng. trans. H. Jacobi. SBE XXII. Oxford, 1884.

Bahuguna, R. P. 1999. "Some Aspects of Popular Movements: Beliefs and Sects in Northern India during the Seventeenth and Eighteenth Centuries." Unpublished PhD dissertation. University of Delhi: Department of History.

——2003a. "Recent Western Writings on Medieval Indian Sant Movement." ICHR Seminar on Dialogue with the Past: Trends in Historical Writings in India, Bangalore, 14–16 February.

——2003b. "Symbols of Resistance: Non-Brahmanical Sants as Religious Heroes in Late Medieval India." In Biswamoy Pati *et al.*, eds., *Negotiating India's Past: Essays in Memory of Parthasarathi Gupta.* Delhi: Tulika Books.

Bakker, Hans. 1986. *Ayodhya.* Groningen: John Benjamins Pub. Co.

Bālarāmāyaṇa, of Rājaśekhara. 1984. Ed. Ganagasagar Rai. Varanasi: Chowkhamba.

Bandhu, Vishva. 1976. *A Vedic Word-Concordance*, I, pt. 1 (1976) and II, pt. 1 (1973). Hoshiarpur: Vishveshvaranand Vedic Research Institute.

Banerji, S. C. 1962. *Dharma-Sūtras: A Study in their Origin and Development.* Calcutta: Punthi Pustak.

Basham, A. L. 1948. "Harṣa of Kashmir and the Iconoclast Ascetics." *Bulletin of the School of Oriental and African Studies* 12/3-4: 688–91.

——1951. *History and Doctrines of the Ājīvikas.* London: Luzac & Company.

——1996. *The Wonder That Was India.* Delhi: Rupa & Co.

Baudhāyana Gṛhyasūtra. 1920. Ed. R. Shama Sastri. 2nd edn. Mysore: Oriental Library Publications.

Bayly, Susan. 2004. "Imagining 'Greater India': French and Indian Visions of Colonialism in the Indic Mode." *Modern Asian Studies* 38/3: 703–744.

Beal, Samuel. 1969. *Si-Yu-Ki: Buddhist Records of the Western World.* Delhi: Munshiram Manoharlal.

Besant, Annie. 1910. *Sanātanadharma: An Elementary Text-book of Hindu Religion and Ethics.* Benares: Central Hindu College.

Bhagavadgītā (*Gītā*). 1988. Text with Eng. trans. Swami Tapasyananda. Madras: Sri Ramakrishna Math.

Bhāgavata Purāṇa. 1315. BS. Ed. Panchanan Tarkaratna. Calcutta: Vangavasi Press.

Bharati, A. 1970. "The Hindu Renaissance and its Apolegetic Patterns." *Journal of Asian Studies* 29: 267–87.

Bhatt, Chetan. 2001. *Hindu Nationalism, Ideologies and Modern Myths.* Oxford: Berg.

Bhattacharji, Sukumari. 2000. *The Indian Theogony.* New Delhi: New Penguin Books.

Battacharya, Ranjana. 1998. "Religion in Early Medieval Gujarat (AD 600–1300)." Unpublished PhD dissertation. University of Delhi: Department of History.

Bhattacharya, Taranath Tarkavacaspati. 1962. *Vācaspatyam.* Reprint. Varanasi: Chowkhamba.

Bhattacharyya, N. N. 1982. *History of Tantric Religion.* Delhi: Manohar.

Bidwai, Praful. 2003. "Storm over move to ban cow killings." *Asia Times* (19 August).

Bloomfield, M. 1908. *Religion of the Veda.* New York and London: G. P. Putnam's Sons.

Bose, Sugata. 1997. "Nation as Mother: Representations and Contestations of 'India' in Bengali Literature." In Sugata Bose and Ayesha Jalal, eds., *Nationalism, Democracy and Development: State and Politics in India.* Delhi: Oxford University Press.

Brahamāṇḍapurāṇa. 1983–84. Trans. and annotated, Ganesh Vasudeo Tagare. Delhi: Motilal Banarsidass.

Brekke, Torkel. 2002. *Makers of Modern Indian Religion in the Nineteenth Century.* New York: Oxford University Press.

Bṛhadāraṇyaka Upaniṣad. 1991. In S. Radhakrishnan, *The Principal Upaniṣads.* Delhi: Oxford University Press.

Bṛhaspatismṛti. 1941. Ed. K. V. Rangaswami Aiyangar. Baroda: Gaekwad Oriental Series.

Brockington, John. 1998. *The Sanskrit Epics.* Leiden: E. J. Brill.

Brown, C. Mackenzie. 1986. "Purāṇas as Scripture: From Sound to Image of the Holy Word in the Hindu Tradition." *History of Religions* 26: 68–86.

Brown, W. Norman. 1957. "The Sanctity of the Cow in Hinduism." *Madras University Journal* 28/2: 29–49.

——1966. *Man in the Universe.* Berkeley: University of California Press.

Bruner-Lachaux, Helene, ed. and trans. 1963–77. *Somaśambhūpaddhati,* 3 parts. Pondicherry: Institute Francais d'Indologie.

Chakrabarti, D. K. 1999. *India: An Archaeological History.* Delhi: Oxford University Press.

Chakrabarti, Kunal. 1995. "Recent Approaches to the Study of Religion in Ancient India." In Romila Thapar, ed., *Recent Perspectives on Early Indian History.* Bombay: Popular Prakashan.

——2001. *Religious Process: The Purāṇas and the Making of a Regional Tradition.* Delhi: Oxford University Press.

Chakraborty, Haripada. 1973. *Asceticism in Ancient India.* Calcutta: Punthi-Pustak.

Chakravarti, Mahadev. 1979. "Beef-Eating in Ancient India." *Social Scientist* 7/11 (June): 51–55.

Champakalakshmi, R. 1978. "Religious Conflict in the Tamil Country." *Journal of the Epigraphical Society of India* 4: 69–81.

Chanana, Dev Raj. 1965. "The Sanskritist and Indian Society." *Enquiry*. New Series. Monsoon. II/2: 49–67.

Chandogya Upaniṣad. 1991. In S. Radhakrishnan, *The Principal Upaniṣads*. Delhi: Oxford University Press.

Chapple, Christopher Key, and John Casey. 2004. *Reconciling Yoga: Haribhadra's Collection of Views on Yoga with a new translation of Haribhadra's Yogadṛṣṭisamuccaya*. Albany: SUNY Press.

Chattopadhyaya, Aparna. 1966. "Martial Life of Brāhmaṇas in Early Medieval India." *Journal of the Oriental Institute* 16: 52–59.

Chattopadhyaya, B. D. 1998. *Representing the Other: Sanskrit Sources and the Muslims*. Delhi: Manohar.

Chattopadhyaya, Debiprasad. 1959. *Lokāyata*. Delhi: People's Publishing House.

Chaudhuri, Nirad C. 1965. *The Continent of Circe*. London: Chatto and Windus.

Choudhary, R. K. 1964. *Vrātyas in Ancient India*. Varanasi: Chowkhamba.

Clark, Mathew. 2006. *The Daśanāmī Sanyāsīs: The Integration of Ascetic Lineages*. Leiden: E. J. Brill.

Cohn, Bernard S. 1987. *An Anthropologist among the Historians and Other Essays*. Delhi: Oxford University Press.

Cort, John, ed. 1998. *Open Boundaries: Jain Communities and Cultures in Indian History*. Albany: SUNY Press.

Crooke, W. 1912. "The Veneration of the Cow in India." *Folklore* XXIII: 275–306.

——(1894) 1978. *The Popular Religion and Folklore of Northern India*. 2 vols. 4th reprint. Delhi: Munshiram Manoharlal.

Cūlavaṃsa. 1996. Trans. Wilhelm Geiger. 1st Indian edn. Delhi: Motilal Banarsidass,

Dalmia, Vasudha. 1995."The Only Real Religion of the Hindus: Vaisnava Self-Representation in the Late Nineteenth Century." In Vasudha Dalmia and Heinrich von Stietencron, eds., *Representing Hinduism: The Construction of Religious Traditions and National Identity*, 176–210. New Delhi: Sage.

——1997. *Nationalisation of Hindu Traditions: Bharatendu Harishchandra and Nineteenth Century Benaras*. Delhi: Oxford University Press.

Danielou, A. 1964. *Hindu Polytheism*. New York: Parthenon.

Das, A. C. 1971 [1920]. *Ṛgvedic India*. Calcutta: University of Calcutta.

Daśāvatāracarita of Kṣemendra. 1891. Ed. Pandit Durgaprasada and Kashinath Panduran Parab. Kavyamālā no. 26. Bombay. Reprint, Delhi: Munshiram Manoharlal, 1983.

Davidson, Ronald M. 2002. *Indian Esotetic Buddhism: A Social History of Tantric Movement*. New York: Columbia University Press.

Davis, Richard H. 1998a. "A Brief History of Religions in India." In Donald S. Lopez, Jr, ed., *Religions of India in Practice*. Indian reprint, Delhi: Munshiram Manoharlal.

——1998b. "The Story of the Disappearing Jains: Retelling the Saiva-Jaina Encounter in Medieval South India." In John Cort, ed., *Open Boundaries: Jain Communities and Cultures in Indian History*. Albany: SUNY Press.

——1999. *Lives of Indian Images*. Delhi: Motilal Banarsidass.

Derrett, J. D. M. 1976–78. *Essays in Classical and Modern Hindu Law*. 4 vols. Leiden: E. J. Brill.

Desai, P. B. 1957. *Jainism in South India and Some Jaina Epigraphs*. Sholapur: Jaina Samskriti Samrakshaka.

Deussen, Paul. 1906. *The Philosophy of the Upaniṣads*. Edinburgh: T&T Clark.

Devīpurāṇa. 1384. BS. Ed. Panchanan Tarkaratna and Srijib Nyayatirth. Calcutta: Navabharat Publishers.

Dhammapada. 1960. Ed. Shri Satkari Sharma Vangiya. Hindi trans. Kancchedilal Gupta. 4th edn. Varanasi: Chowkhamba Vidyabhavan.

Dharmapradīpa. 1937. Ananta Kṛṣṇa Śāstrī, Sītarāma Śāstrī and Śrījīva Bhaṭṭacārya, Calcutta.

Dharmattvavinirṇaya. 1929. Vāsudev Śāstrin Abhyaṅkara, Poona.

Dīghanikāya. 1958. 3 vols. Ed. Bhikhu Jagdish Kassapa, Bihar Government. Nalanda-Devanagari-Pali Series. Patna: Pali Publication Board. Eng. trans. T. W. Rhys Davids, *The Dialogues of the Buddha*, 3 vols. London: Pali Text Society, 1889–1921.

Divyāvadāna. 1886. Ed. E. B. Cowell and A. B. Neil. Cambridge: Cambridge University Press.

Doniger (O'Flaherty), Wendy. 1971. "The Origin of Heresy in Hindu Mythology." *History of Religions* 10 (May): 271–333.

——1975. *Hindu Myths*. Baltimore: Penguin.

——1983. "The Image of the Heretic in the Gupta Purāṇas." In Bardwell L. Smith, ed., *Essays on Gupta Culture*. Delhi: Motilal Banarsidass.

——1988. *The Origin of Evil in Hindu Mythology*. Delhi: Motilal Banarsidass.

——1991."Hinduism by Any Other Name." *Wilson Quarterly* (Summer): 35–41.

Dumont, L. 1988. *Homo Hierachicus*. New Delhi: Oxford University Press.

Dundas, Paul. 1992. *The Jains*. London and New York: Routledge.

Dvyāśrayakāvya of Hemacandra. 1915–21. Ed. Abhaya-Tilaka Gani and Abaji Vishnu Kathavate. Bombay: Government Central Press.

Einoo, S. 1996. "The Formation of the Pūjā Ceremony." In Hanns-Peter Schmidt and Albrecht Wezler, eds., *Veda-Vyākaraṇa-Vyākhyāna: Festschrift Paul Thieme zum 90*, 73–87. Reinbek: Verlag fur Orientalistische Fachpublikationen.

Ernst, Carl. W. 2004. *Eternal Garden: Mysticism, History, and Politics at a South Asian Sufi Center*. Delhi: Oxford University Press.

Falk, H. 1982. "Zur Tierzucht Im Alten Indien." *Indo-Iranian Journal* 24: 169–80.

Farmer, Steve, and Michael Witzel. 2004. "The Collapse of the Indus-Script Thesis: The Myth of a Literate Harappan Civilization." *Electronic Journal of Vedic Studies* 11/2: 19–57.

Farquhar, J. N. 1925a. "The Organization of the Sannyasis of the Vedānta." *Journal of the Royal Asiatic Society* (July): 479–86.

——1925b. "The Fighting Ascetics of India." *Bulletin of the John Rylands Library* 9: 431–52.

Flood, Gavin, ed. 2003. *The Blackwell Companion to Hinduism*. Indian reprint. Kundli (Haryana): Replika Press.

——2004. *An Introduction to Hinduism*. 1st South Asian edition. Delhi: Foundation Books.

Friedmann, Yohanan. 1975. "Muslim Views of Indian Religions." *Journal of the American Oriental Society* 95/2: 214–21.

Frietag, Sandria B. 1996. "Contesting in Public: Colonial Legacies and Contemporary Communalism." In David Ludden, ed., *Making India Hindu.* Delhi: Oxford University Press.

Frykenberg, Robert. 1997. "The Emergence of Modern 'Hinduism' as a Concept and as an Institution." In Günther-Dietz Sontheimer and Hermann Kulke, eds., *Hinduism Reconsidered*, 82–107. Delhi: Manohar.

Gandhi, M. K. (1927) 2000. *An Autobiography or The Story of My Experiments with Truth.* Ahmedabad: Navajivan Trust.

Ghosh, A., ed. 1975. *Jaina Art and Architecture.* 2 vols. Delhi: Bharatiya Jnanapith.

Ghurye, G. S. 1964. *Indian Sadhus.* Bombay: Popular Prakashan.

Gītagovindam. 2000. Ed. and trans. N. S. R. Ayengar. Delhi: Penman Publishers.

Gobhila Gṛhyasūtra. 1992. Ed. with Hindi trans. Thakur Udaya Narain Singh. Delhi: Chowkhamba. Eng. trans. H. Oldenberg. SBE XXIX. Oxford, 1886.

Golwalkar, M . S. 1939. *We or Our Nationhood Defined.* Nagpur: Bharat Publications.

——1966. *Bunch of Thoughts.* Bangalore: Sahitya Sindhu Prakashan.

Golzio, Karl-Heinz. 1990. "Das Problem von Toleranz und Intoleranz in indischen Religionen anhand epigraphischer Quellen." In Helmut Eimer, ed., *Frank-Richard Hamm Memorial Volume*, 89–102. Bonn: Indica et Tibetica Verlag.

Gonda, J. 1965. *Change and Continuity in Indian Religion.* The Hague: Mouton & Co.

——1976. *Viṣṇuism and Śivaism: A Comparison.* Delhi: Munshiram Manoharlal.

——1977. *The Ritual Sūtras.* Wiesbaden: Otto Harrassowitz.

——1980. *Vedic Ritual: The Non-Solemn Rites.* Leiden: E. J. Brill.

Gopal, Ram. 1959. *India of Vedic Kalpasūtras.* Delhi: National Publishing House.

Gopatha Brāhmaṇa of the Atharva Veda. 1972. Ed. Rajendra Lal Mitra. Reprint. Delhi: Indological Book House.

Goswami, Manu. 2004. *Producing India.* Delhi: Permanent Black.

Goudriaan, Teun, and Sanjukta Gupta. 1981. *Hindu Tantric and Śākta Literature.* Wiesbaden: Otto Harrassowitz.

Granoff, Phyllis. 1984. "Holy Warriors: A Preliminary Study of Some Biographies of Saints and Kings in the Classical Indian Tradition." *Journal of Indian Philosophy* 12: 291–303.

——1991–92. "Tolerance in the Tantras: Its Form and Function." *Journal of Indian Philosophy* 46-47: 283–302.

Grimes, John A. 2005. "Darśana." In Sushil Mittal and Gene Thursby, eds., *The Hindu World.* New York and London: Routledge.

Gross, Robert Lewis. 1992. *The Sadhus of India.* Jaipur: Rawat Publications.

Guha, Sudeshna. 2005. "Negotiating Evidence: History, Archaeology and the Indus Civilisation." *Modern Asian Studies* 39/2: 399–426.

Gupta, S. P. 1996. *The Indus-Saraswati Civilization: Origins, Problems and Issues.* Delhi: Pratibha Prakashan.

——2000–2001. Review of B. B. Lal's *The Saraswati Flows On. Puratattva* 31: 189–90.

Habib, Irfan. 1994. *Linguistic Materials from Eighth-Century Sind: An Exploration of the Chachnama*, Symposia Papers 11. Aligarh: Indian History Congress.

——1999. "The Envisioning of a Nation: A Defence of the Idea of India." *Social Scientist* 27/9-10: 18–29.

——2001. "Imagining River Saraswati—A Defence of Commonsense." *Proceedings*, Indian History Congress. 61st session. Kolkata: 65–92.

Habib, Irfan, ed., 2005. *India: Studies in the History of an Idea.* Delhi: Munshiram Manoharlal.

Hacker, Paul. 1957. "Religiose Toleranz und Intoleranz in Hinduism." *Saeculum* 8: 167–79.

——1978. "Der religiose Nationalismus Vivekanandas." In L. Schmithausen, ed., *Kleine Schriften.* Wiesbaden: Steiner.

Haider, Najaf. 2005. "A 'Holi Riot' of 1714: Versions from Ahmadabad and Delhi." In Mushirul Hasan and Asim Roy, eds., *Living Together Separately: Cultural India in History and Politics.* Delhi: Manohar.

Halbfass, Wilhelm. 1990. *India and Europe: An Essay in Philosophical Understanding.* Delhi: Motilal Banarsidass.

——1991. *Tradition and Reflection: Exploration in Indian Thought.* Albany: SUNY Press.

Haṃsayogin. 1917. *Sanātanadharmadīpikā.* Madras.

Harṣacarita of Bāṇa. 1961. Trans. E. B. Cowell and F. W. Thomas. Delhi: Motilal Banarsidass.

Hasan, Mushirul. 1996. " The Myth of Unity: Colonial and National Narratives." In David Ludden, ed., *Making India Hindu.* New Delhi: Oxford University Press.

Hatcher, Brian A. 1999. *Eclecticism and Modern Hindu Discourse.* New York: Oxford University Press.

Haṭhayogapradīpikā of Svātmarāman, with the commentary of Brahmānanda. 1972. Ed. and trans. Srinivasa Iyengar. Madras: Adyar Library and Research Centre.

Hauer, J. W. 1961. *Toleranz und Intoleranz in den nichtchristlichen Religionen.* Stuttgart: W. Kohlhammer.

Hawley, John Stratton. 1991. "Naming Hinduism." *Wilson Quarterly* (Summer): 20–32.

Hazra, R. C. 1958–63. *Studies in the Upapurāṇas.* 2 vols. Calcutta: Sanskrit College.

——1975. *Studies in the Puranic Records on Hindu Rites and Customs.* Delhi: Motilal Banarsidass.

Heesterman, J. C. 1957. *The Ancient Indian Royal Consecration.* The Hague: Mouton.

——1962–63. "Vrātya and Sacrifice." *Indo-Iranian Journal* 6: 1–37.

——1984."Non-Violence and Sacrifice." *Indologica Taurinensia* XII: 119–27.

——1985. *The Inner Conflict of Tradition.* Delhi: Oxford University Press.

——1993. *The Broken World of Sacrifice: An Essay in Ancient Indian Ritual.* Chicago: University of Chicago Press.

Hiraṇyakeśī Gṛhyasūtra. 1929. Anandashrama Sanskrit Granthavali no. 53. Eng. trans. H. Oldenberg. SBE XXIX. Oxford, 1886.

Holt, John Clifford. 2004. *The Buddhist Visnu: Religious Transformation, Politics, and Culture.* New York: Columbia University Press.

Hopkins, E. W. 1931. "The Divinity of Kings." *Journal of the American Oriental Society* 51: 309–316.

Hussain, Anwar. 1993. "The 'Foreigners' and the Indian Society: c. Eighth Century to Thirteenth Century." Unpublished M. Phil. dissertation. Delhi: Jawaharlal Nehru University.

Islam, Shamsul. 2006. Golwalkar's *We or Our Nationhood Defined: A Critique with the Text of the Book.* New Delhi: Pharos Media and Publishing.

Ivanow, W. 1936. "The Sect of Imam Shah in Gujrat." *Journal of the Bombay Branch of the Royal Asiatic Society* 12: 19–70.

Jaffrelot, Christophe. 1996. *The Nationalist Movement and Indian Politics 1925 to the 1990s.* Delhi: Penguin Books India.

Jaffrelot, Christophe, ed. 2005. *The Sangh Parivar: A Reader.* Delhi: Oxford University Press.

——2007. *Hindu Nationalism: A Reader.* Delhi: Permanet Black.

Jaina Purāṇa Kośa (in Hindi). 1993. Ed. Pravin Chandra Jain and Darbarilal Kothia. Srimahavirji, Rajasthan: Jain Vidya Samsthan.

Jaina Rājataraṅgiṇī of Śrīvara. 1977. With translation, critical introduction and geographical notes. Ed. Raghunath Singh. Varanasi: Chowkhamba.

Jaini, P. S. 2000. *Collected Papers on Jaina Studies.* Delhi: Motilal Banarsidass.

——2001. *Collected Papers on Buddhist Studies.* Delhi: Motilal Banarsidass.

Jaiswal, Suvira. 1981. *Origin and Development of Vaiṣṇavism.* 2nd revised and enlarged edn. Delhi: Munshiram Manoharlal.

——1991. "Semitising Hinduism: Changing Paradigms of Brahmanical Integration." *Social Scientist* 19/12 (December): 20–32.

Jambūddivpaññattisuttam. 1986. Ed. Kanhailalji Kamal *et al.* Vyavara, Rajasthan: Shri Agam Prakashan Samiti.

Jamison, Stephanie W. 1991. *The Ravenous Hyenas and the Wounded Sun.* Ithaca, NY and London: Cornell University Press.

Jesudasan, C., and H. Jesudasan. 1961. *A History of Tamil Literature.* Calcutta: YMCA Publishing House.

Jha, D. N. 2002. *The Myth of the Holy Cow.* London: Verso.

——2004. *The Early India: A Concise History.* Delhi: Manohar.

——2006. *Looking for a Hindu Identity (General President's Address).* Visva Bharati: Indian History Congress.

Jones, K. 1981. "Religious Identity and the Indian Census." In N. G. Barrier, ed., *The Census in British India.* Delhi: Manhar.

Jordens, J. T. F. 1978. *Dayanand Saraswati: His Life and Ideas.* Delhi: Oxford University Press.

Joshi, Laxman Sastri. 1972. "Was the Cow Killed in Ancient India?" *Quest* 75: 83–87.

Kādambarī of Bāṇa. 1968. Ed. and trans. M. R. Kale. Delhi: Motilal Banarsidass.

Kaiwar, Vasant. 2003. "The Aryan Model of History and the Oriental Renaissance: The Politics of Identity in an Age of Revoutions, Colonialism, and Nationalism." In Vasant Kaiwar and Sucheta Mazumdar, eds., *Antinomies of Modernity: Essays on Race, Orient, Nation.* Delhi: Tulika Books.

Kane, P. V. 1974. *History of Dharmaśāstra.* 5 vols. 2nd edn. Poona: Bhandarkar Oriental Research Institute.

Kanungo, Pralay. 2002. *RSS'S Tryst With Politics: From Hedgewar to Sudarshan.* Delhi: Manohar.

Kapiṣṭhala Kaṭha Saṃhitā. 1968. Ed. Raghu Vira. 2nd edn. Delhi: Meharchand Lachhmandas.

Kāṭhaka Gṛhyasūtra. 1925. Ed. W. Caland. Lahore: Research Department, D. A. V. College.

Kāṭhaka Saṃhitā. 1970–1972. Ed. Leopold von Schroeder and Richard Simon. Wiesbaden: Franz Steiner Verlag.

Kaṭha Upaniṣad. 1991. In S. Radhakrishnan, *The Principal Upaniṣads.* Delhi: Oxford University Press.

Kathāsaritasāgara of Somadeva. 1960. Ed. and trans. Kedarnath Sharma. Patna: Bihar Rashtra Bhasha Parisad.

Kauśika Sūtra of the Atharvaveda (1890) 1972. Ed. M. Bloomfield. *Journal of the American Oriental Society* 14. Delhi: Motilal Banarsidass.

Kauśitaka Gṛhyasūtra. 1944. Ed. T. R. Chintamani. Madras: Madras University.

Kauṣītaki Upaniṣad. 1991. In S. Radhakrishnan, *The Principal Upaniṣads.* Delhi: Oxford University Press.

Keith, A. B. (1925) 1970. *The Religion and Philosophy of the Veda and Upanisads.* Harvard Oriental Series. Indian reprint. Delhi: Motilal Banarsidass.

Keralotpatti. 1961. Ed. Herman Gundert. Trivandrum: Balan Publications.

Khādira Gṛhyasūtra. 1934. Ed., trans. and published by Thakur Udaya Narayana Singh. Muzaffarpur. Eng. trans. H. Oldenberg, SBE XXIX. Oxford, 1886.

Killingley, Dermot. 1993. *Rammohun Roy in Hindu and Christian Tradition.* Newcastle upon Tyne: Grevatt & Grevatt.

——2003. "Modernity, Reform, and Revival." In Gavin Flood, ed., *The Blackwell Companion to Hinduism.* Indian reprint. Kundli (Haryana): Replika Press.

King, Richard. 1999. *Orientalism and Religion.* Oxford and Delhi: Oxford University Press.

Klostermaier, Klaus K. 1979. "Hindu Views of Buddhism." In Roy C. Amore, ed., *Developments in Buddhist Thought: Canadian Contributions to Buddhist Studies.* Ontario: Canadian Corporation for Studies in Religion.

——1990. *A Survey of Hinduism.* Delhi: Munshiram Manoharlal.

——1991. "The Original Dakṣa Saga." In Arvind Sharma, ed., *Essays on the Mahābhārata.* Leiden: E. J. Brill.

Kolhatkar, M. B. 1999. *Surā: The Liquor and the Vedic Sacrifice.* New Delhi: D. K. Printworld.

Kosambi, D. D. 1962. *Myth and Reality.* Bombay: Popular Prakashan.

Kṛtyakalpataru, Niyatakālakāṇḍam, tṛtīyabhāgam. 1950. Ed. K. V. Rangaswami Aiyangar. Baroda: Oriental Research Institute.

Kulārṇava Tantra. (1965) 1975. Ed. Tārānāth Vidyāratna with an introduction by Arthur Avalon. Madras: Ganesh & Company. Reprint, Delhi: Motilal Banarsidass.

Kulke, Hermann. 1993. *Kings and Cults: State Formation and Legitimation in India and Southeast Asia.* Delhi: Manohar.

Kunjan Pillai, Elamkulam P. N., ed. 1955. *Candrotsavam.* Kottayam: National Book Stall.

Kuvalayamālā of Udyottanasūri, Part I. 1959. Ed. A. N. Upadhye. Bombay: Bharatiya Vidya Bhavan.

Lal, B. B. 1960. "From the Megalithic to the Harappa: Tracing Back the Graffiti on the Pottery." *Ancient India* 16: 4–24.

——1997. *The Earliest Civilization of South Asia: Rise, Maturity and Decline.* Delhi: Aryan Books International.

——1998. "Rigvedic Aryans: The Debate Must Go On." *East and West* 48/3-4 (December): 439–48.

——2002. *The Saraswatī Flows On.* Delhi: Aryan Books International.

Lal, Makhan, *et al.* 2002. *India and the World for Class VI* (September). New Delhi: National Council of Educational Research and Training,

Lawrence, Bruce B. 1976. *Shahrastānī on the Indian Religions.* The Hague: Mouton.

Lee, Kwangsu. 2003. "Resisting Analysis, Persisting Interpretation: A Historiography of Some Recent Studies of Hinduism in the United States." *Social Science Probings* 15/3-4 (Winter): 11–28.

Lincoln, Bruce. 1982. *Priests, Warriors and Cattle.* Berkeley and Los Angeles: University of California Press.

Lipner, Julius. 1994. *Hindus: Their Religious Beliefs and Practices.* London: Routledge.

——(2004) 2005. "On Hinduism and Hinduisms: The Way of the Banyan." In Sushil Mittal and Gene Thursby, eds., *The Hindu World.* New York: Routledge. Indian reprint, Kundli (Haryana): Replika Press.

Llewellyn, J. E. 1993. *The Arya Samaj as a Fundamentalist Movement.* Delhi: Manohar.

Long, Jeffery D. 2007. *A Vision for Hinduism: Beyond Hindu Nationalism.* London and New York: I. B. Tauris.

Lorenzen, David N. 1978. "Warrior Ascetics in Indian History." *Journal of the American Oriental Society* 98: 61–75.

——1999. "Who Invented Hinduism?" *Comparative Studies in Society and History* 41/4 (October): 630–59.

——2006. *Who Invented Hinduism?: Essays on Religion in History.* Delhi: Yoda Press.

Lorenzen, D., ed. 1996. *Bhakti Religion in North India: Community Identity and Political Action.* Albany: SUNY Press.

Macdonell, A. A. 1897. *Vedic Mythology.* Strassburg: K. J. Trubner. Indian reprint, Varanasi: Indological Book House, 1963.

Macdonell, A. A., and A. B. Keith. 1912. *Vedic Index of Names and Subjects.* 2 vols. London: John Murray. Reprint, Varanasi: Motilal Banarsidass, 1958.

Maclean, Derryl N. 1989. *Religion and Society in Arab Sind.* Leiden: E. J. Brill.

Mahalingam, T. V. 1954. *South Indian Polity.* Madras: University of Madras.

Mahāvaṃsa. 1958. Ed. W. Geiger. London: Pali Text Society and Luzac & Co. Trans. W. P. Anand Guruge. Calcutta: M. P. Birla Foundation, 1990.

Mahāvīracarita. 1973. Ed. and trans. Rampratap Tripathi Shastri. Allahabad: Lok Bharati Prakashan.

Maitrayāṇī Saṃhitā. 1881–86. Ed. Leopold von Schroeder. 4 vols. Leipzig: F. A. Brockhaus.

Maitrāyaṇīya Upaniṣad. 1991. In S. Radhakrishnan, *The Principal Upaniṣads*. Delhi: Oxford University Press.

Malalasekera, G. P. 1983. *Dictionary of Pāli Proper Names*. 2 vols. 1st Indian Edition. Delhi: Munshiram Manoharlal.

Malamoud, Charles. 1996. *Cooking the World: Ritual and Thought in Ancient India*. Delhi: Oxford University Press.

Manusmṛti or *Mānava Dharmaśāstra*. 1886. Ed. V. N. Mandlika. Bombay: Ganpat Krishnaji's Press. Eng. trans. G. Bühler. SBE XXV. Oxford, 1921.

Margul, Tadeusz. 1968. "Present-Day Worship of the Cow in India." *Numen* 15/1 (February): 63–80.

Marshall, P. J. 1970. *The British Discovery of Hinduism in the Eighteenth Century*. London: Cambridge University Press.

Matsyapurāṇa. 1970. Ed. Acharya Ram Sharma. Bareli: Sanskriti Sansthan.

Matsyapurāṇam. 1981. Anandasrama Sanskrit Series. Poona.

Mattavilāsa Prahasana of Mahendravikramavarman. 1973. Ed. and trans. N. P. Unni. Trivandrum: College Book House.

Mayrhofer, Manfred A. 1956–80. *A Concise Etymological Dictionary*. 4 vols. Heidelberg: Carl Winter, Universitatsverlag. Revised edition, *Etymologisches Wörterbuch des Altindoarischen*, 3 Baender. Heidelberg: Carl Winter, Universitatsverlag, 1986–89.

McCutcheon, Russell T. 2003. *Manufacturing Religion: The Discourse on Sui Generis Religion and the Politics of Nostalgia*. New York: Oxford University Press.

Meghadūta Kālidāsa. 1979. Ed. and trans. M. R. Kale. Delhi: Motilal Banarsidass.

Meinhard, H. 1928. *Beiträge zur Kenntnis des Śivaismus nach den Purāṇa's*. Thesis. Bonn: University of Bonn.

Michaels, Axel. 2005. *Hinduism: Past and Present*. Delhi: Orient Longman.

Minor, Robert N. 1982. "Sarvepalli Radhakrishnan on the Nature of 'Hindu' Tolerance." *Journal of the American Academy of Religion* 50/2: 275–90.

——1991. *Modern Indian Interpreters of the Bhagavadgītā*. Delhi: Sri Satguru Publications.

Mishra, Manisha. 2003. "Perception of the Hindus and their Religious Systems as Described in the *Dabistan-i-Mazahib*." M.Phil. dissertation. University of Delhi: Department of History.

Misra, Amalendu. 2004. *Identity and Religion: Foundations of anti-Islamism in India*. New Delhi: Sage Publications.

Misra, R. N. 1997. "Pontiffs' Empowerment in Central Indian Śaivite Monachism." *Journal of the Asiatic Society of Bombay* 72: 72–86.

Mitra, R. L. (1881) 1969. *The Indo-Aryans: Contributions to the Elucidation of Ancient and Medieval History*. 2 vols. Calcutta: W. Newman. Reprint, Varanasi: Indological Book House.

Mittal, Sushil, and Gene Thursby, eds. 2004. *The Hindu World.* London/New York: Routledge.

Monier-Williams, Monier. 1963. *Sanskrit-English Dictionary.* Delhi: Motilal Banarsidass.

Mukherjee, B. N. 2001. *Nationhood and Statehood in India: A Historical Survey.* New Delhi: Regency Publications.

Mukherjee, S. N. 1968. *Sir William Jones: A Study in Eighteenth-Century British Attitudes to India.* Cambridge: Cambridge University Press.

Muṇḍaka Upaniṣad. 1991. In S. Radhakrishnan, *The Principal Upaniṣads.* Delhi: Oxford University Press.

Naiṣadhacarita of Śrī Harṣa. 1965. Trans. with commentaries K. K. Handiqui. Poona: Deccan College.

Naiṣadhamahākāvyam. 1981. Ed. Haragovind Shastri. Varanasi: Chowkhamba.

Nandi, R. N. 1986. *Social Roots of Religion in Ancient India.* Calcutta: K. P. Bagchi.

——2000. "Origin of the Vīraśaiva Movement." In D. N. Jha, ed., *The Feudal Order.* Delhi: Manohar.

Narain, A. K. 1983. "Religious Policy and Toleration in Ancient India with particular reference to the Gupta Period." In Baldwell L. Smith, ed., *Essays on Gupta Culture.* Delhi: Motilal Banarsidass.

Narang, S. P. 1972. *Hemacandra's Dvyāśrayakāvya: A Literary and Cultural Study.* Delhi: Munshiram Manoharlal.

Narayanan, M. G. S. 1970. "Kantallur Salai—New Light on the Nature of Aryan Expansion to South India." *Proceedings of the Indian History Congress.* Jabalpur Session.

Nath, Vijay. 2001. *Purāṇas and Acculturation: A Historico-Anthropological Perspective.* Delhi: Munshiram Manoharlal.

Nehru, Jawaharlal. 1946. *The Discovery of India.* Calcutta: Signet Press.

Nilakanta Sastri, K. A. 1975. *The Coḷas.* Madras: University of Madras.

——1987. *A History of South India.* Delhi: Oxford University Press.

Nītivākyamṛtam of Somadeva Sūri. 1987. Ed. and trans. Sudhir Kumar Gupta. Jaipur: Prakrita Bharati Academy.

Nyāyakusumāñjali of Udayanācārya, vol. 1. 1996. Trans. N. S. Dravid. New Delhi: Indian Council of Philosophical Research.

Oberhammer, G. 1983. *Inklusivismus. Eine indische Denkform.* Vienna: Institüt für Indologie der Universitat Wein.

Oberoi, Harjot. 1994. *The Construction of Religious Boundaries: Culture, Identity and Diversity in the Sikh Tradition.* Delhi: Oxford University Press.

O'Connell, Joseph T. 1973. "The Word 'Hindu' in Gauḍīya Vaiṣṇava Texts." *Journal of the American Oriental Society* 93/3: 340–43.

Oldenberg, Herman. 1912. *Ṛgveda: Textkritische und exegetische Noten.* Berlin: Weidmannsche Buchhandlung.

Olivelle, Patrick. 2002. *Food for Thought: Dietary Rules and Social Organization in Ancient India.* Amsterdam: Royal Netherlands Academy of Arts and Sciences.

Orr, W. G. 1940. "Armed Religious Ascetics in Northern India." *Bulletin of the John Rylands Library* 24: 81–100.

Padmapurāṇa. 1893–94. Ed. Hari Narayan Apte. Anandasrama Sanskrit Series. Poona.

Palapiyūṣalatā. Saṃvat 1951. Darbhanga: Gouriśayantrālaya.

Pandey, G. C. 1994. *Life and Thought of Śaṅkarācārya*. Delhi: Motilal Banarsidass.

Pāraskara Gṛhyasūtra. 1991. Ed. Jagdish Chandra Mishra. Varanasi: Chowkhamba. Eng. trans. H. Oldenberg. SBE XXIX. Oxford, 1886.

Parpola, Asko. 1994. *Deciphering the Indus Script*. Cambridge: Cambridge University Press.

Pennington, Brian K. 2005. *Was Hinduism Invented? Britons, Indians and the Colonial Construction of Religion*. New York: Oxford University Press.

Periyapurāṇam of Śekkilār. 1990. Eng. trans. T. N. Ramachandran. Thanjavur: Tamil University.

Peterson, Indira Viswanathan. 1989. *Tevāram. English* (Poems to Śiva). Princeton: Princeton University Press.

——1998. "Śramaṇas Against the Tamil Way." In John Cort, ed., *Open Boundaries: Jain Communities and Cultures in Indian History*. Albany: SUNY Press.

Pinch, William R. 1996. *Peasants and Monks in British India*. Berkeley: California University Press.

Prabodhacandrodaya of Kṛṣṇa Miśra. 1998. Ed. and trans. Sita Nambiar. Delhi: Motilal Banarsidass.

Prasad, Ganga. 1909. *The Fountainhead of Religion*. Reprint, San Diego: The Book Tree, 2000.

Pratimānāṭakam of Bhāsa. 1983. Ed. M. R. Kale. Delhi: Motilal Banarsidass.

Prinja, Nawal K. 1996. *Explaining Hindu Dharma: A Guide for Teachers*. Norwich: Vishwa Hindu Parishad (UK).

Proudfoot, I. 1987. *Ahiṃsā and a Mahābhārata Story*. Canberra: Australian National University.

Rādhākānta Deva. 1886. *Śabdakalpadruma*. 5 vols. Calcutta: Baptist Mission Press. Reprint, Delhi: Nag Publishers, 1987.

Rājataraṅgiṇī of Jonarāja. 1972. Ed. and trans. Raghunath Singh. Varanasi: Chowkhamba.

Rājataraṅgiṇī of Kalhaṇa. 1979–1988. 3 vols. Trans. with an introduction, commentary and appendices, M. A. Stein. Delhi: Motilal Banarsidass.

Ram, L. L. Sundara. 1927. *Cow Protection in India*. Madras: The South Indian Humanitarian League, George Town.

Ramachandran, Rajesh. 2000. "A Crisis of Identity." *The Hindustan Times*, 7 May.

Ramaswamy, Sumathi. 2003. "The Goddess and the Nation: Subterfuges of Antiquity, the Cunning of Modernity." In Gavin Flood, ed., *The Blackwell Companion to Hinduism*. Indian reprint, Kundli (Haryana): Replika Press.

Rao, Velcheru Narayana. 1990. *Śiva's Warriors: The Basava Purāṇa of Pālkuriki Somanātha*. Princeton: Princeton University Press.

Ray, Rajat Kanta. 2004. *The Felt Community: Commonality and Mentality before the Emergence of Indian Nationalism*. New Delhi: Oxford University Press.

Reddy, C. Rammanohar. 2001. “Intolerance of Food Habits.” *The Hindu:* 16 September.

Renou, Louis. 1965. *The Destiny of the Veda in India.* English trans. Dev Raj Chanana. Delhi: Motilal Banarsidass.

——1971. *Vedic India.* Indian reprint, Varanasi: Indological Book House.

Ṛgveda. 1877. Ed. Theodor Aufrecht. *Die Hymnen des Rigveda,* 2 Bde. 2. Auflge. Bonn: A. Marcus. German trans. K. Fiedrich Geldner, 1951–1957. *Der Rigveda.* Harvard Oriental Series XXXIII–XXXVI. Cambridge, MA: Harvard University Press.

Rocher, Ludo. 1986. *The Purāṇas.* Wiesbaden: Otto Harassowitz.

Rolland, Romain. 1988. *The Life of Vivekanada and the Universal Gospel.* Calcutta: Advaita Ashrama.

Sachau, Edward C. 1910. *Alberuni's India.* London: K. Paul, Trench, Trybner & Co.

Sadasivaiah, H. M. 1967. *A Comparative Study of Two Vīraśaiva Monasteries.* Mysore: University of Mysore.

Sankalia, H. D. 1967. “(The Cow) in History.” *Seminar* (May): 93.

Sāṅkhyāyana Gṛhyasūtra. 1960. Ed. S. R. Sehgal. Delhi: Munshiram Mnoharlal. Eng. trans. H. Oldenberg. SBE XXIX. Oxford, 1886.

Sarkar, Jadunath. 1958. *A History of Dasnami Naga Sanyasis.* Allhabad: Mahanirvani.

——1919 (1973). *Shivaji and His Times.* Calcutta: Orient Longman.

Sarkar, Tanika. 1996. “Imaginning Hindurashtra: The Hindu and the Muslim in Bankim Chandra's Writings.” In David Ludden, ed., *Making India Hindu.* Delhi: Oxford University Press.

Sarup, Lakshman. 1984. *The Nighaṇṭu and the Nirukta.* Indian edition, Delhi: Motilal Banarsidass.

Sarva-darśaṇa-saṃgraha. 1914. Trans. E. B. Cowell and A. E. Gough. London: Kegan Paul, Trench, Trubner & Co.

Sastri, Ajay Mitra, ed. 1995. *Inscriptions of the Sarabhapurias, Pāṇḍuvamśins and Somavams ins.* Delhi: Indian Council of Historical Research & Motilal Banarsidass.

Sastri, H. Krishna. 1946. *Memoirs of the Archaeological Survey of India,* vol. 26. Calcutta: Central Publication Branch, Govt of India. Reprint, Delhi: Swati Publications, 1991.

Śatapatha Brāhmaṇa. 1855. Ed. Albrecht Weber. Berlin: Ferd. Dummler's Verlagsbuchhandlung. Eng. trans. Julius Eggeling. 5 vols. SBE XII, XXVI, XLI, XLIII, XLIV. Oxford, 1882–1900.

Sathe, Shanta. 1994. *Lokmanya Tilak: His Social and Political Thoughts.* Delhi: Ajanta.

Ṣaṭsāhasra Saṃhitā. 1982. Ed. and trans. J. A. Schoterman. Leiden: E. J. Brill.

Saurapurāṇa. 1924. Ed. V. G. Apte. Anandasrama Sanskrit Series. Poona.

Savarkar, V. D. 2005 [1923]. *Hindutva: Who is a Hindu?* Delhi: Hindi Sahitya Sadan.

Schmidt, Hans-Peter. 1968. “The Origin of Ahiṃsā.” *Mèlanges d'Indianisme à la mémoire de Louis Renou.* Paris: Editions E. de Boccard.

Sen, Amartya. 2005. *The Argumentative Indian.* London: Allen Lane.

Sharma, Arvind. 1978. "Some Misunderstandings of the Hindu Approach to Religious Plurality." *Religion* 8: 133–54.
——1983. *Studies in "Alberuni's India".* Wiesbaden: Otto Harrassowitz.
——2002. "Of Hindu, Hindustān, Hinduism and Hindutva." *Numen* 49: 1–36.
Sharma, Arvind, ed. 2003. *The Study of Hinduism.* Columbia: University of South Carolina Press.
Sharma, B. N. 1970. "Religious Tolerance and Intolerance as Reflected in Indian Sculptures." *Journal of the Ganganth Jha Research Institute.* Umesh Mishra Commemoration Volume: 655–66.
Sharma, R. S. 1974. "Material Milieu of Tantricism." In R. S. Sharma, ed., *Indian Society: Historical Probings* (In Memory of D. D. Kosambi). Delhi: People's Publishing House.
——1983. *Material Culture and Social Formations in Ancient India.* Delhi: Macmillan.
——1990. "Communalism and India's Past." *Social Scientist* 18/1-2 (January-February): 3–12.
——1994. *Looking for the Aryans.* Hyderabad: Orient Longman.
——1999a. *Advent of the Aryans in India.* Delhi: Manohar.
——1999b. "Identity of the Indus Culture." *East and West* 49/1-4 (December): 35–45.
——2000. *Communal History and Rāma's Ayodhya.* Delhi: People's Publishing House.
Sharma, Shanta Rani. 1996. *Society and Culture in Rajasthan c. AD 700–900.* Delhi: Pragati Prakashan.
Shastri, Rajnikant. 1988. *Hindu Jāti Kā Utthān aur Patan.* Allahabad: Kitab Mahal.
Shende, N. J. 1985. *The Religion and Philosophy of the Atharvaveda.* Poona: Bhandarkar Oriental Research Institute.
Shri Bharat Dharma Mahamandala. 1924. *The World's Eternal Religion.* Benares: Bharat Dharma Syndicate.
Shrimali, K. M. 2003. "Constructing an Identity: Forging Hinduism into Harappan Religions." *Social Science Probings* 15/1-2: 1–59.
Shulman, David Dean. 1985. *The King and the Clown in South Indian Myth and Poetry.* Princeton: Princeton University Press.
Simoons, Frederick J. 1979. "Questions in the Sacred-Cow Controversy." *Current Anthropology* 20/3 (September): 467–76.
——1994. *Eat Not This Flesh.* Madison: University of Wisconsin Press.
Singh, S. D. 1965. *Ancient Indian Warfare with special reference to the Vedic Period.* Leiden: E. J. Brill.
Sircar, D. C. 1960. *Studies in the Geography of Ancient and Medieval India.* Delhi: Motilal Banarsidass.
——1965. *Select Inscriptions Bearing on Indian History and Civilization*, vol. 1. Calcutta: Calcutta University.
——1971. *Studies in the Religious Life in Ancient and Medieval India.* Delhi: Motilal Banarsidass.
Śivapurāṇa. 1314. BS. Ed. Panchanan Tarkaratna. Calcutta: Vangavasi Press.
Skanda Purāṇa. 1986–87. 7 vols. Delhi: Nag Publishers.

Smith, Brian K. 1989. *Reflections on Resemblance, Ritual and Religion*. New York: Oxford University Press.

——1990. "Eaters, Food, and Social Hierarchy in Ancient India." *Journal of the American Academy of Religion* LVIII/2: 177–206.

Sontheimer, Günther-Dietz. 1997. *King of Hunters, Warrriors and Shepherds*. Delhi: Manohar.

Sontheimer, Günther-Dietz and Hermann Kulke, eds. 1997. *Hinduism Reconsidered*. Delhi: Manohar.

Sorensen, S. 1963. *An Index to the Names in the Mahābhārata*. Delhi: Motilal Banarsidas.

Śrīmad Śaṅkaradigvijayam by Vidyāraṇya. 2 vols. Eng. trans. K. Padmanaban. Madras: Padmanaban, 1985–86.

Srinivasan, Doris. 1979. *Concept of Cow in the Ṛgveda*. Delhi: Motilal Banarsidass.

Srivastava, A. L. 1984. *The Sultanate of Delhi (711–1526)*. Agra: Shivalal Agrawal & Company.

Srivastava, S. K. 1989. *Sir Jadunath Sarkar: The Historian at Work*. Delhi: Anamika Prakashan.

Staal, Frits. 1979. "The Concept of Scripture in the Indian Tradition." In Mark Juergensmeyer and Gerald Barrier, eds., *Sikh Studies: Comparative Perspectives on a Changing Tradition*. Berkeley: Graduate Theological Union.

——1989. *Rules Without Meaning: Ritual, Mantras and the Human Sciences*. New York: Peter Lang.

Stanley, John M. 1990. "The Capitulation of Maṇi: A Conversion Myth in the Cult of Khaṇḍobā." In Alf Hiltebeitel, ed., *Criminal Gods and Demon Devotees*. Delhi: Manohar.

Śvetāśvatara Upaniṣad. 1991. In S. Radhakrishnan, *The Principal Upaniṣads*. Delhi: Oxford University Press.

Sweetman, Will. 2003. *Mapping Hinduism: Hinduism and the Study of Indian Religions 1600–1776*. Halle: Verlag der Franckeschen Stiftungen zu Halle.

Taittirīya Āraṇyaka of the Black Yajurveda with the commentary of Sāyaṇācārya. 1872. Ed. R. L. Mitra. Calcutta: Asiatic Society.

Tiattirīya Brāhmaṇa with the commentary of Sāyaṇācārya. 1979. Ed. Narayana Sastri Godabole. 3 vols. 3rd edn. Anandashramagranthavali no. 37. Poona.

Taittirīya Saṃhitā. 1871–72. Ed. Albrecht Weber. 2 vols. Leipzig: F. A. Brockhaus. Eng. trans. A. B. Keith, *The Veda of the Black Yajus School entitled Taittirīya Sanhitā*. Cambridge, MA, Harvard University Press, 1914. Reprint, Delhi: Motilal Banarsidass, 1967.

Taittirīya Upaniṣad. 1991. In S. Radhakrishnan, *The Principal Upaniṣads*, Delhi: Oxford University Press.

Takakusu, J., trans. 1966. *A Record of Buddhist Religion as Practised in India and the Malay Archipelago (A.D. 671–695) by I-tsing*. Delhi: Munshiram Manoharlal.

Tāṇḍya Brāhmaṇa with the commentary of Sāyaṇācārya. 1935–36. 2 vols. Kashi Sanskrit Series. Benaras: Haridas Sanskrit Granthmala.

Tarkapancānan, Haracandra. 1940. *Mataparīkṣottaram*. Calcutta: Sumachurn Chandrica.

Tattvasaṃgraha of Śāntarakṣita. 1968. Ed. Dwarkadas Shastri. Varanasi: Bauddha Bharati. Eng. trans. Ganganatha Jha. Gaekwad Oriental Series. Baroda, 1937.

Thakur, Upendra. 1964. *Studies in Jainism and Buddhism in Mithila*. Varanasi: Chowkhamba.

Thapar, Romila. 1987. *Cultural Transaction and Early India: Tradition and Patronage*. Delhi: Oxford University Press.

——1996. "Ideology and the Upanisads." In D. N. Jha, ed., *Society and Ideology in India: Essays in Honour of Professor R. S. Sharma*. Delhi: Munshiram Manoharlal.

——1997. "Syndicated Hinduism." In Günther-Dietz Sontheimer and Hermann Kulke, eds., *Hinduism Reconsidered*. Delhi: Manohar.

——2000. *Cultural Pasts: Essays in Early Indian History*. Delhi: Oxford University Press.

Thite, G. U. 1975. *Sacrifice in the Brāhmaṇa Texts*. Poona: University of Poona.

Tod, James. 1829. *Annals and Antiquities of Rajasthan* 1. London: Smith, Elder and Co. 1st Indian reprint, New Delhi: Oriental Books Reprint Corporation, 1983.

Tsuji, Naoshiro (alias Fukushima). 1952. *On the Relation of Brāhmaṇas and Śrautasūtras* (English summary). Tokyo: The Tôyô Bunko.

Tull, Herman W. 1996. "The Killing that is not Killing: Men, Cattle and the Origins of Non-violence (*Ahiṃsā*) in the Vedic Sacrifice." *Indo-Iranian Journal* 39: 223–44.

Ulrich, Katherine E. 2007. "Food Fights: Buddhist, Hindu and Jain Dietary Polemics in South India." *History of Religions* 46/3: 228–61.

Urban, Hugh B. 2001. *The Economics of Ecstasy*. New York: Oxford University Press.

Uttararāmacarita with notes and the commentary of Ghanaśyāma. 1962. Ed. and trans. P. V. Kane and C. N. Joshi. Delhi: Motilal Banarsidass.

Vaikhānasa Gṛhyasūtra. 1927–29. Ed. W. Caland, Bibliotheca Indica, Calcutta, 1927; text and trans. Asiatic Society, Calcutta.

Varāhapurāṇa. 1313. BS. Ed. Panchanan Tarkaratna. Calcutta: Vangavasi Press.

Vasiṣtha Dharmasutra. 1883. Ed. Alois Anton Fuhrer. Sanskrit and Prakrit Series, 23. Bombay. Eng. trans. G. Bühler. SBE XIV. Oxford, 1882.

Veluthat, Kesavan. 1978. *Brāhmaṇa Settlements in Kerala*. Calicut University: Sandhya Publications.

Viṣṇupurāṇa. 1331. B. S. Ed. Panchanan Tarkaratna. Calcutta: Vangavasi Press.

Viṣṇusmṛti. 1881. Ed. Julius Jolly. Bibliotheca Indica Series. Calcutta: Asiatic Society. Eng. trans. *The Institutes of Viṣṇu*. SBE VII. Oxford, 1880.

Von Stietencron, Heinrich. 1995. "Religious Configurations in Pre-Muslim India and the Modern Concept of Hinduism." In Vasudha Dalmia and H. von Stietencron, eds., *Representing Hinduism*. Delhi: Sage Publications.

——1997. "Hinduism: On the Proper Use of a Deceptive Term." In Günther-Dietz Sontheimer and Hermann Kulke, eds., *Hinduism Reconsidered.* Delhi: Manohar.

Vyākaraṇa Mahābhāṣya of Patañjali. 1962–72. 3 vols. Ed. F. Kielhorn. Poona: Bhandarkar Oriental Research Institute.

Wadekar, M. L. 1996. *Devalasmṛti Reconstruction.* 2 vols. Delhi: Chowkhamba.

Wagoner, Philip B. 1996. "Sultan among Hindu Kings: Dress, Titles, and the Islamicization of Hindu Culture at Vijayanagara." *Journal of Asian Studies* 55/4 (November): 851–80.

White, David Gordon. 2003. *Kiss of the Yogini: "Tantric Sex" in its South Asian Contexts.* Chicago and London: University of Chicago Press.

Witzel, Michael. 1991. "On the Sacredness of the Cow in India." Unpublished manuscript, abridged version published as *Ushi.wo meguru Indojin no kagae* (in Japanese) no. 1: 9–20. The Association of Humanities and Sciences, Kobe Gakuin University.

Witzel, Michael, and Steve Farmer. 2000. "Horseplay at Harappa: The Indus Valley Decipherment Hoax." *Frontline* (13 October and 24 November).

Yadava, B. N. S. 1973. *Society and Culture in Northern India in the Twelfth Century.* Allahabad: Central Book Depot.

Yājñavalkyasmṛti (with the commentary *Bālakrīḍā* of Viśvarūpācārya). 1982. Ed. Mahāmahopādhyāya T. Ganapati Sastri. Delhi: Munshiram Manoharlal. *Yājñavalkyasmṛti* with Vijñāneśvara's Mitakṣarā. Ed. Gangasagar Rai. Delhi: Chowkhamba, 1998.

Yogaśāstra of Hemacandra. 1977. 3 vols. Ed. Muni Jambuvijaya. Mumbai: Jaina Sahitya Vikasa Mandala.

Young, Richard Fox. 1981. *Resistant Hinduism: Sanskrit Sources on Anti-Christian Apologetics in Early Nineteenth Century India.* Vienna: Roberto de Nobili Research Library.

Zagorin, Perez. 2003. *How the Idea of Religious Toleration Came to the West.* Princeton: Princeton University Press.

Zavos, John. 2000. *The Emergence of Hindu Nationalism in India.* Delhi: Oxford University Press.

——2001. "Defending Hindu Tradition: Sanatana Dharma as a Symbol of Orthodoxy in Colonial India." *Religion* 31: 109–123.

Zend Avesta. 1880–87. 3 vols. Eng. trans. James Darmesteter and L. H. Mills. Oxford: SBE IV, XXIII, XXXI.

Zvelebil, Kamil. 1992. *Companion Studies to Tamil Literature.* Leiden: E. J. Brill.

Index